How to Draw Dogs (A how to draw dogs book kids will love)

This book has over 300 detailed illustrations that demonstrate how to easily draw dogs step by step

James Manning

Copyright © 2020

All rights reserved. No part of this publication may be reproduced, stored in a retrieval system, or transmitted in any form or by any means, electronic, mechanical, recording, scanning, or otherwise, except as permitted under copyright legislation, without the prior permission of the authors.

Limits of liability/disclaimer of warranty –

The authors have used their best efforts in preparing this book, they make no representations or warranties with respect to the accuracy or the completeness of the contents of this book and specifically disclaim any implied warranties or merchantability or fitness for a particular purpose. No warranty may be created or extended. The author shall not be liable for any loss or profit or any other commercial damages, including but not limited to special, incidental, consequential or other damages.

Copyright © 2020

1. Drawing a basic grid outline will help you to give your picture good proportions.

You can find all of the grids shown in this book at:

https://www.lipdf.com/product/doggrids/

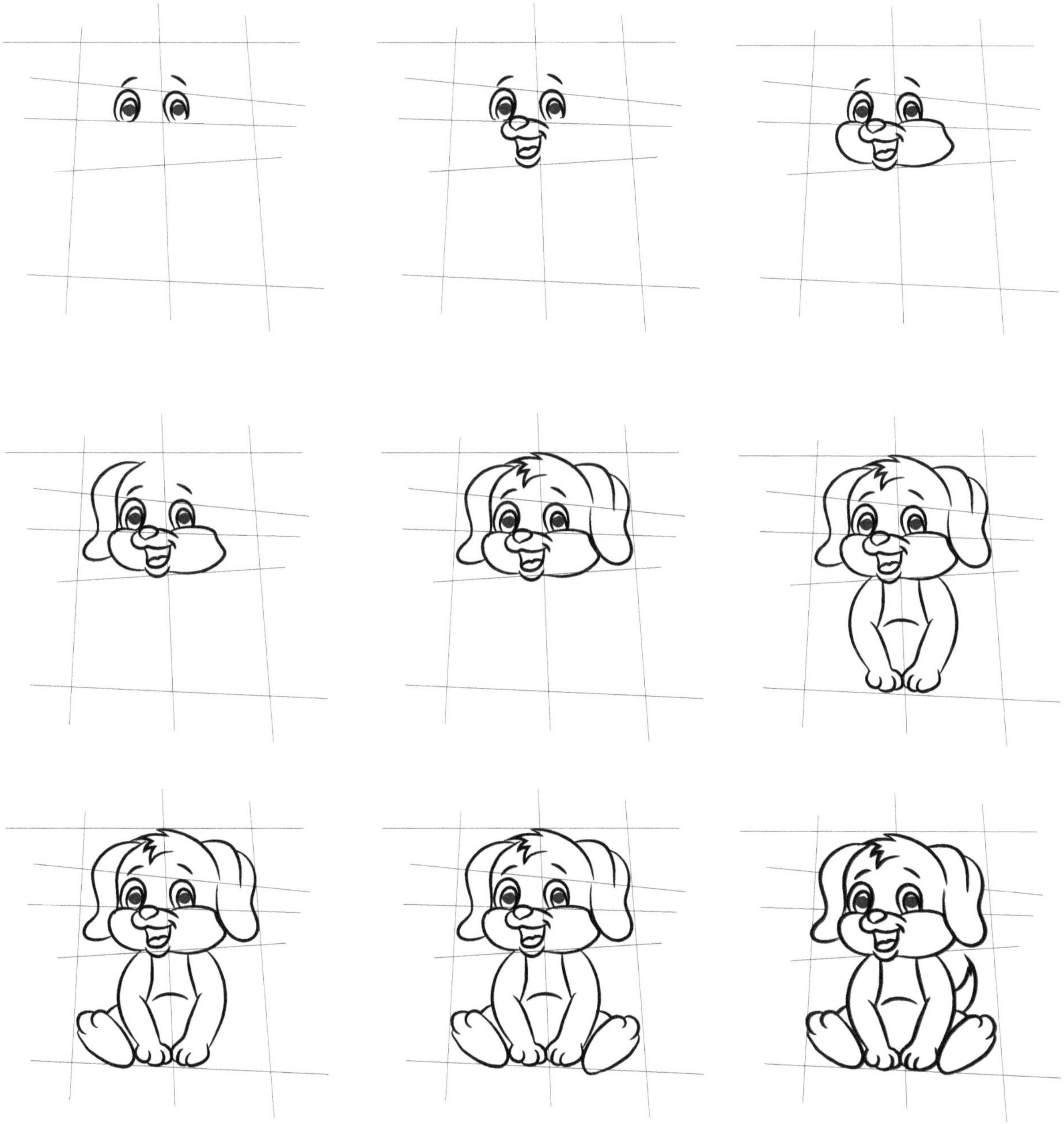

How to draw a dog using a grid. You can download blank grids to practice with in dark and light PDF formats by following the link below.

https://www.lipdf.com/product/grids/

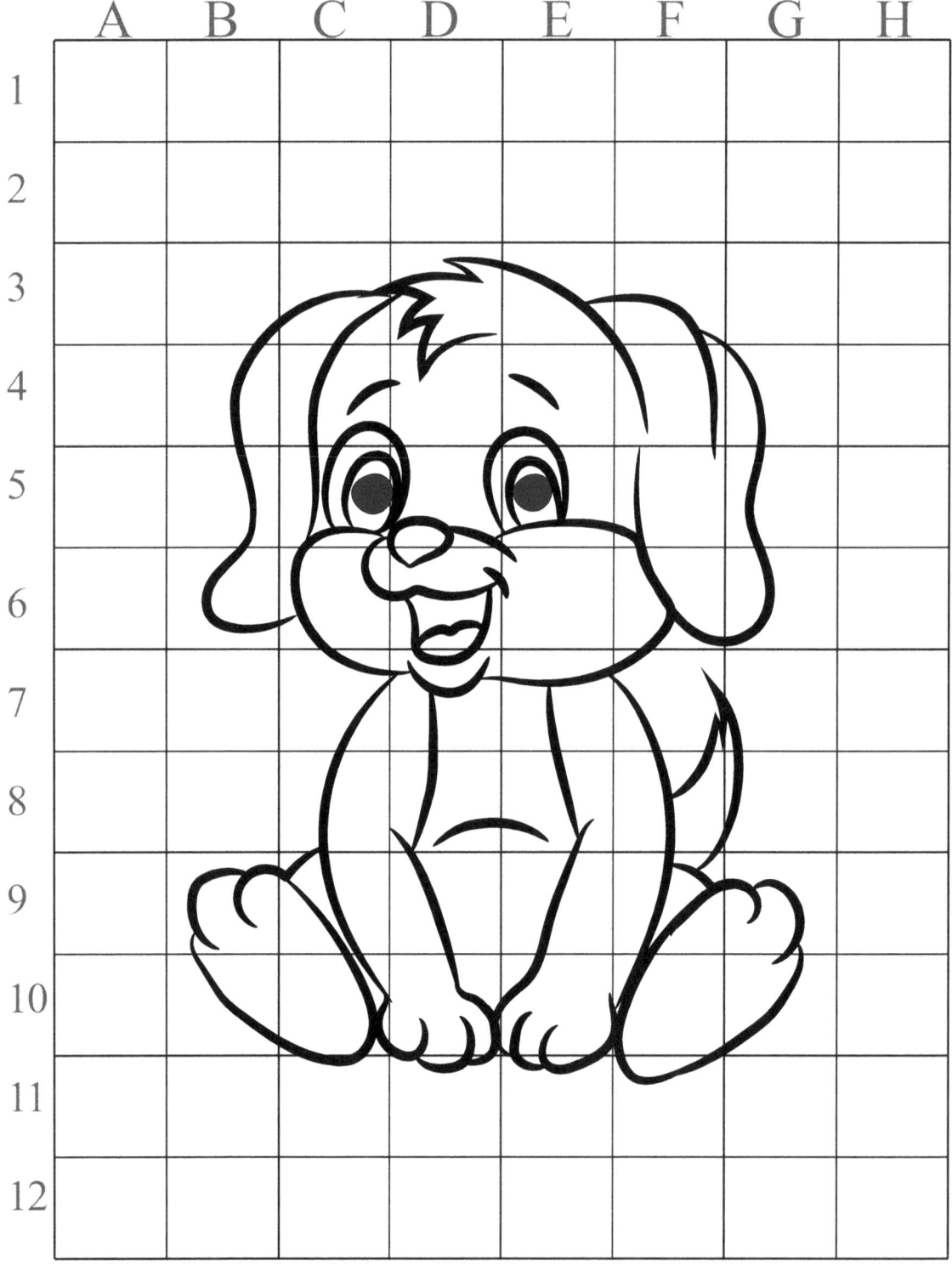

2. Drawing lines on your grid will help you to draw eyes that are focused on a distant object.

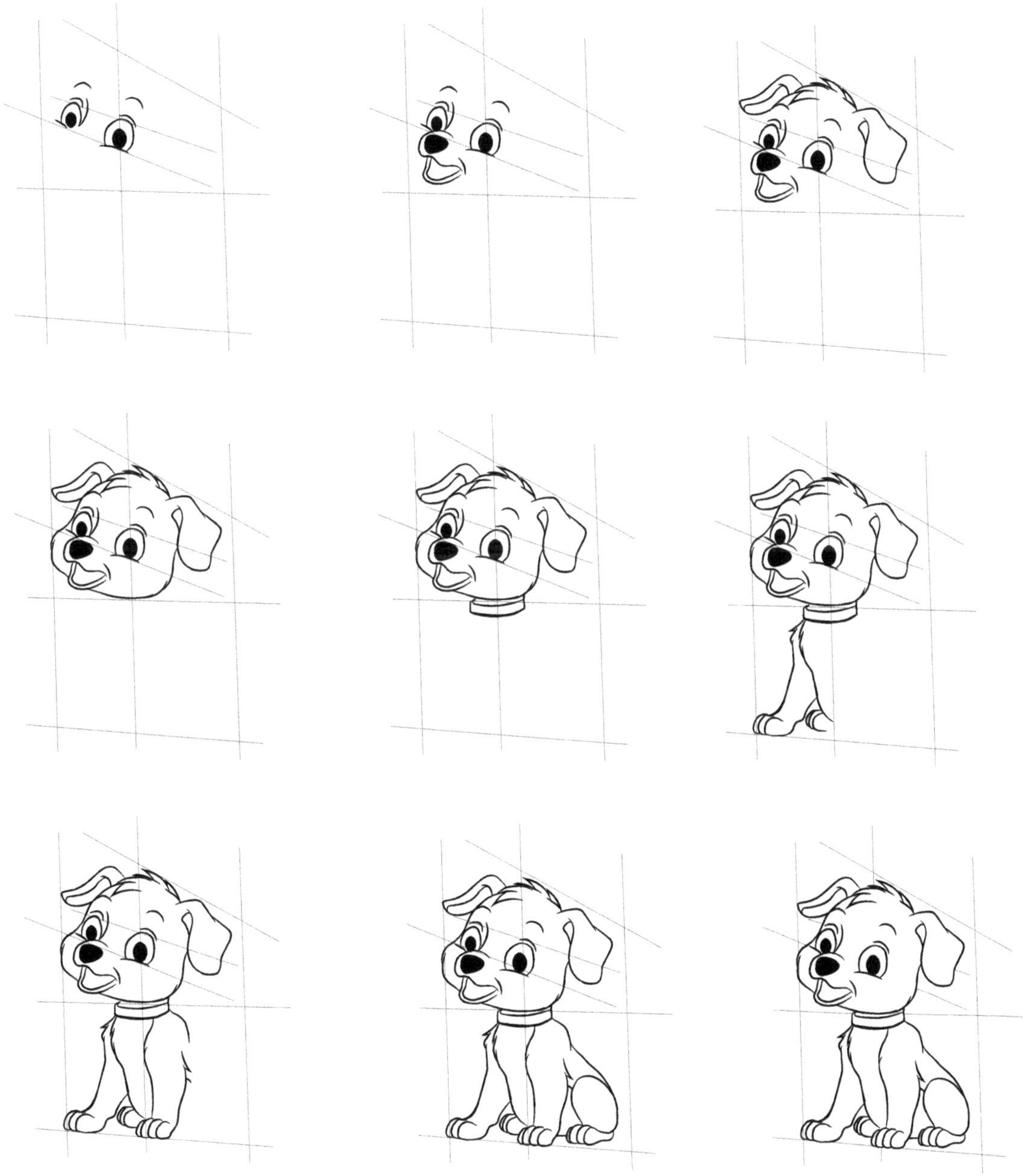

How to draw a dog using a grid. You can download blank grids to practice with in dark and light PDF formats by following the link below.

https://www.lipdf.com/product/grids/

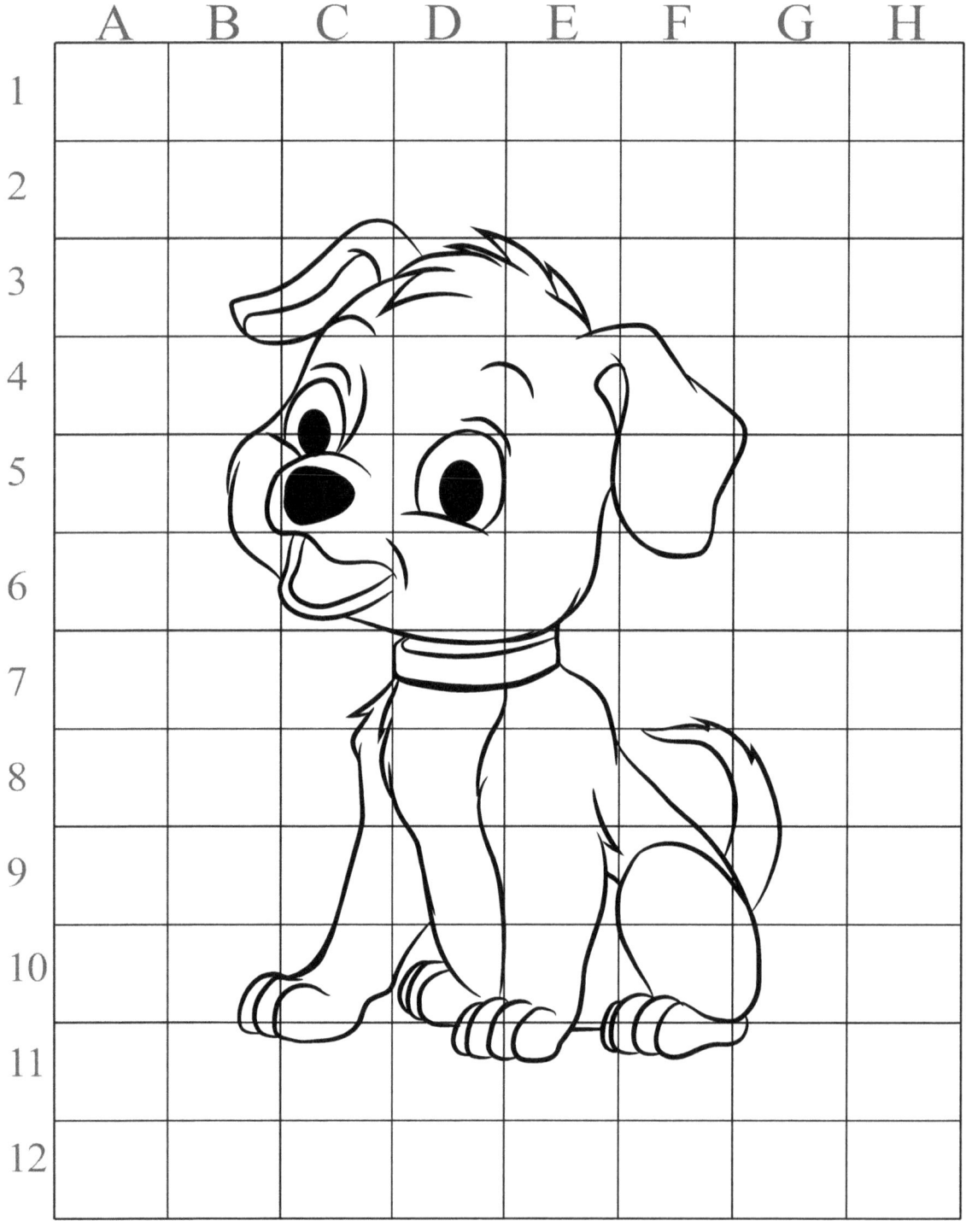

3. Starting your drawing with the eyes will help your initial sketch to take shape.

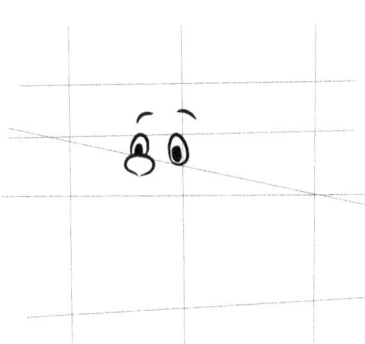 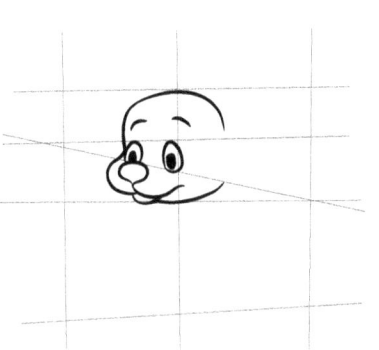 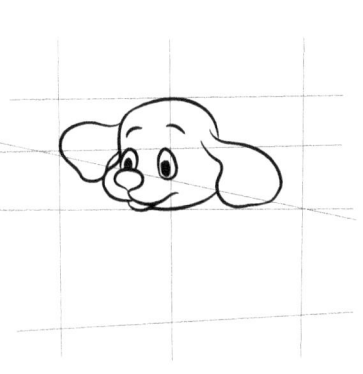

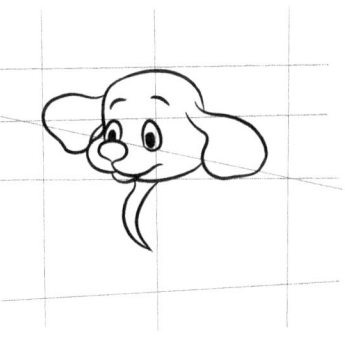  

How to draw a dog using a grid. You can download blank grids to practice with in dark and light PDF formats by following the link below.

https://www.lipdf.com/product/grids/

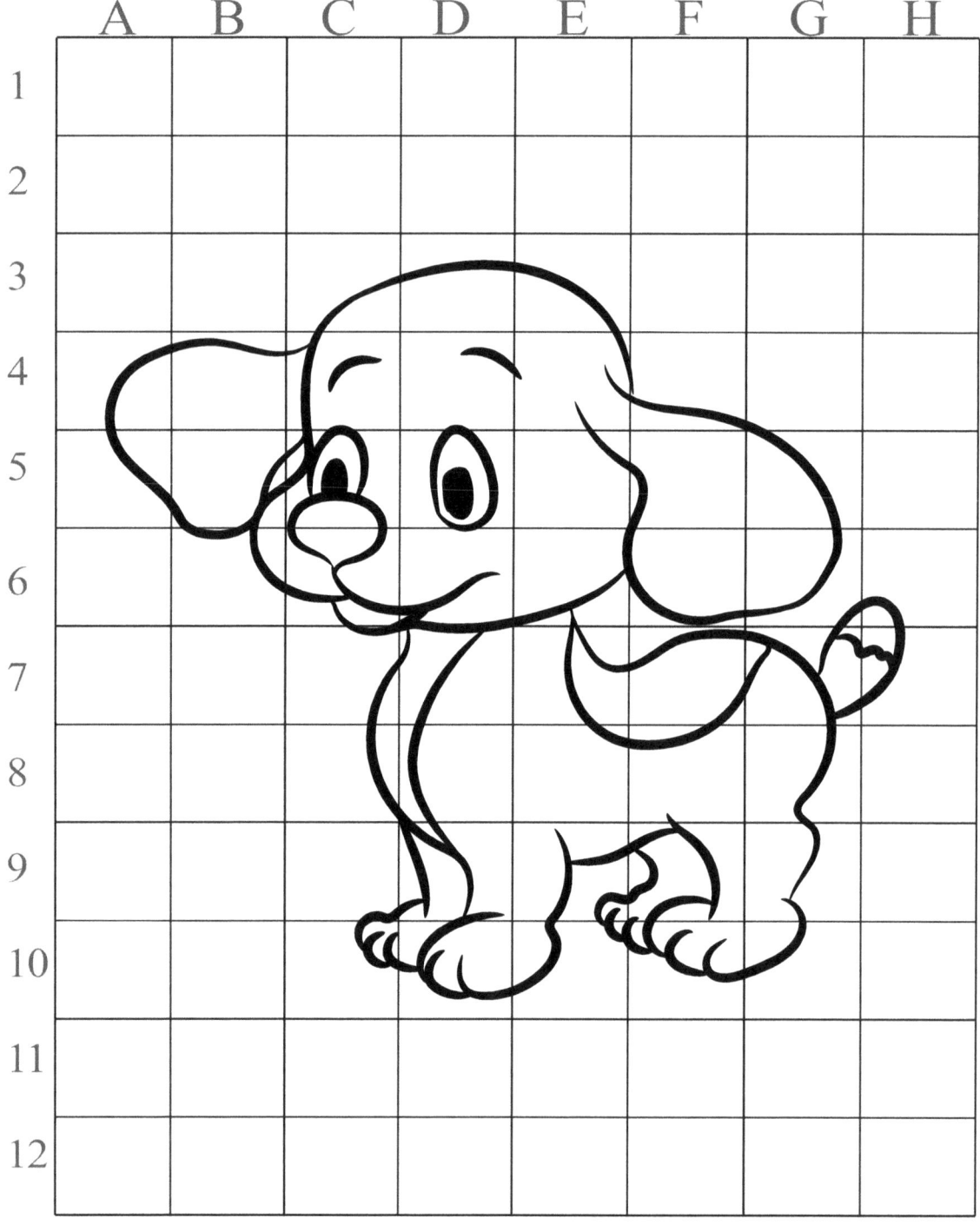

4. You can develop the direction the head of your drawing takes with the use of a few carefully positioned lines on your grid.

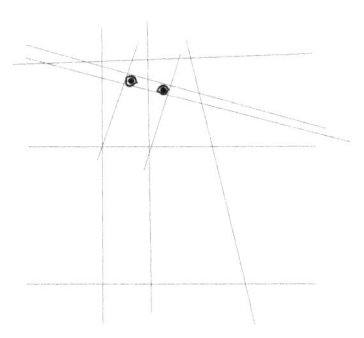 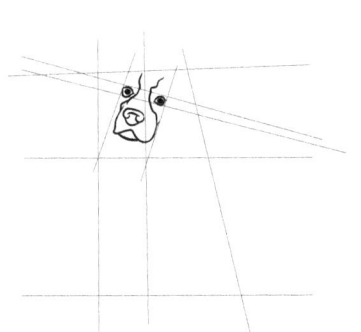 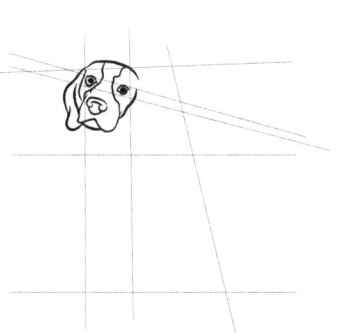

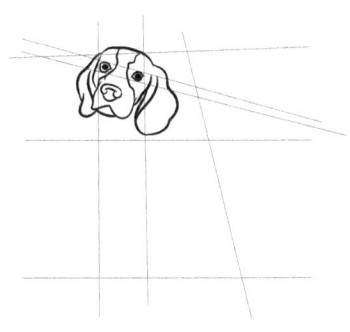  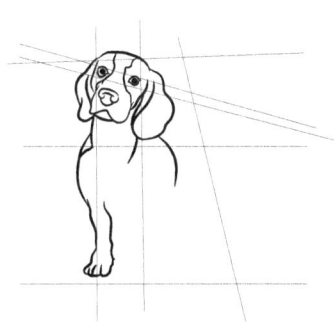

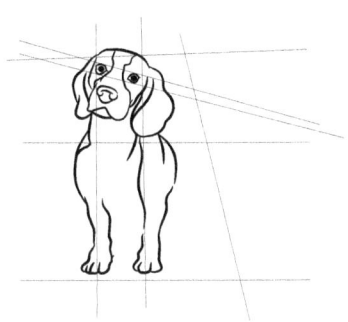 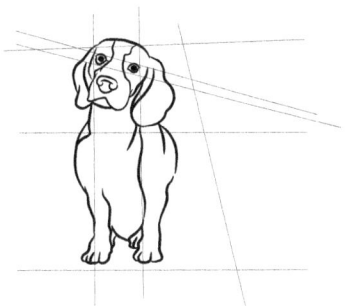 

How to draw a dog using a grid. You can download blank grids to practice with in dark and light PDF formats by following the link below.

https://www.lipdf.com/product/grids/

5. Start your drawing with the eyes and construct a face around it next.

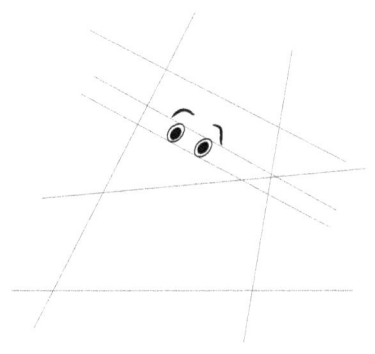
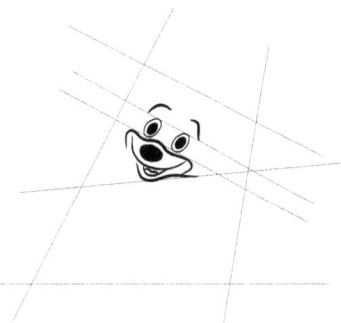

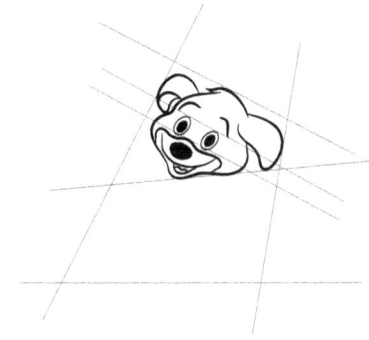

How to draw a dog using a grid. You can download blank grids to practice with in dark and light PDF formats by following the link below.

https://www.lipdf.com/product/grids/

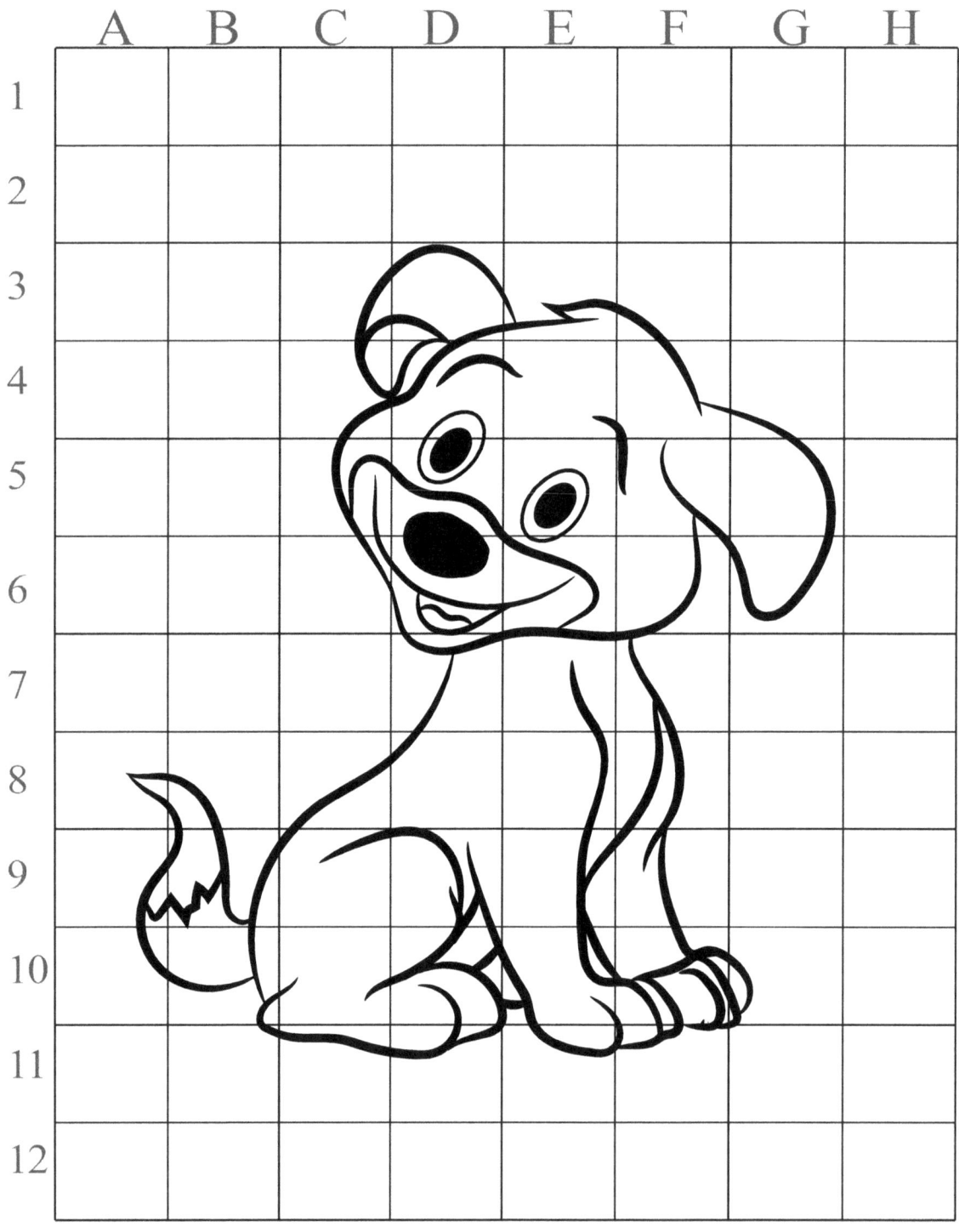

6. Separate your grid into sections to help you decide how you want to proportion your drawing.

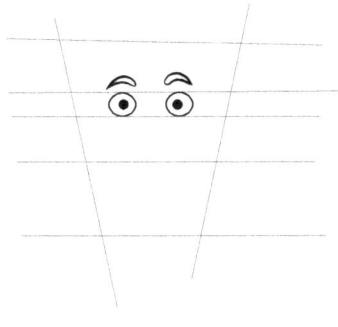
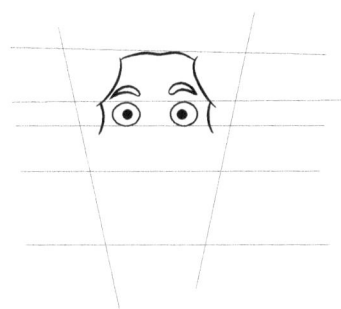

How to draw a dog using a grid. You can download blank grids to practice with in dark and light PDF formats by following the link below.

https://www.lipdf.com/product/grids/

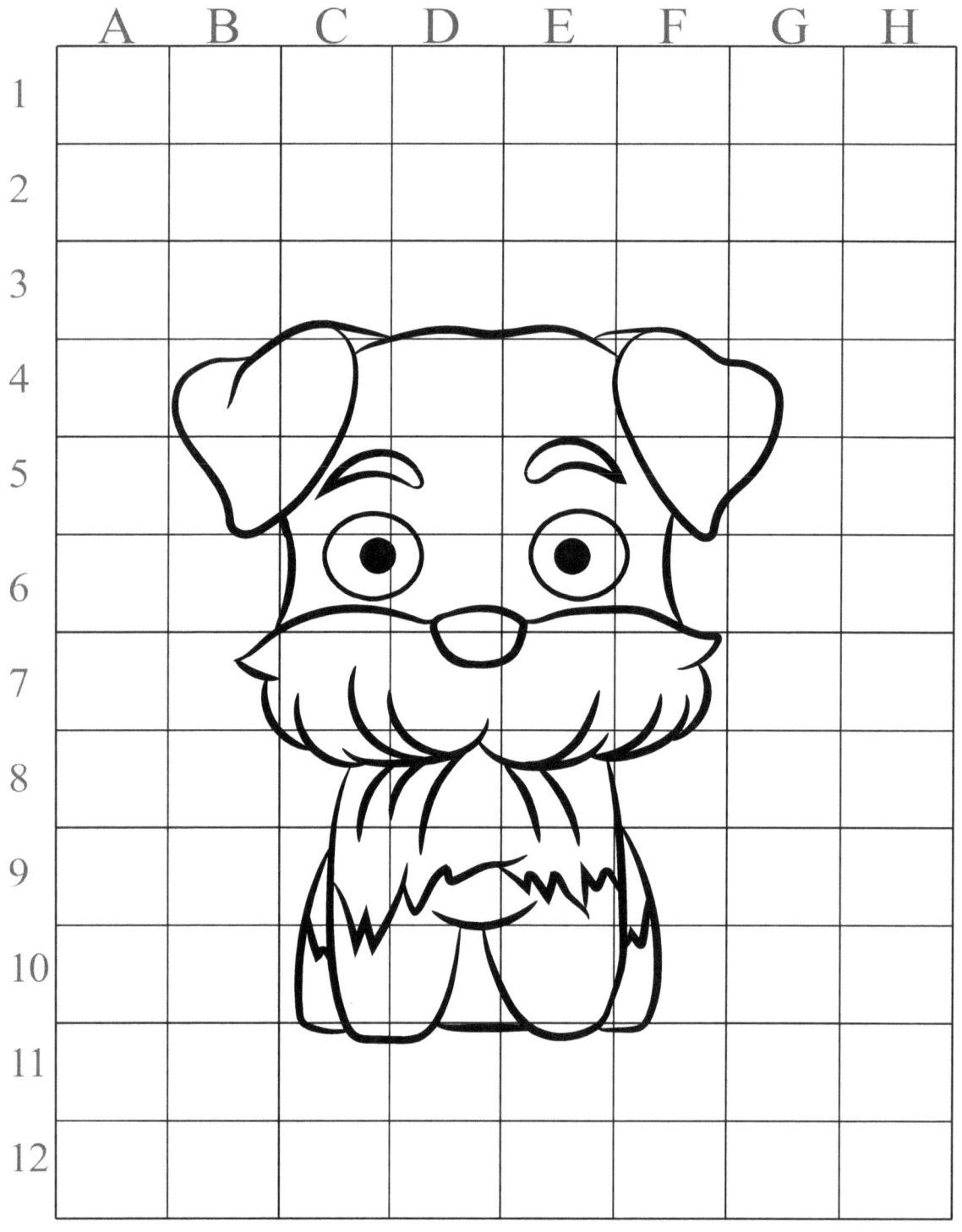

7. Draw the head first and then build the rest of the body around it.

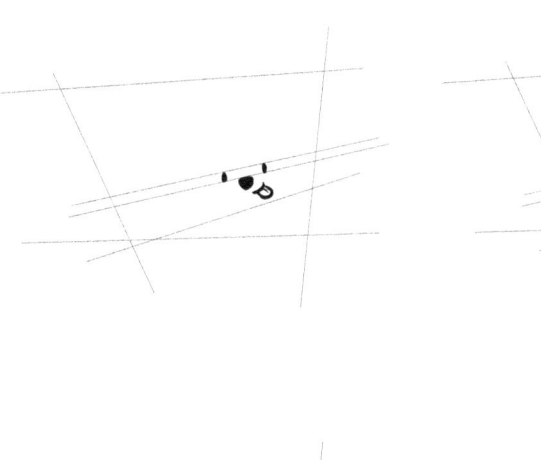
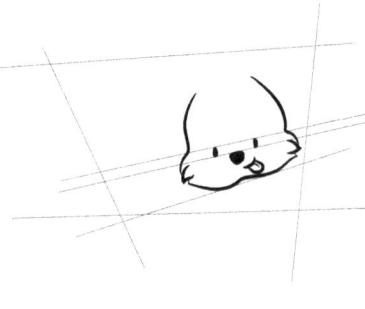
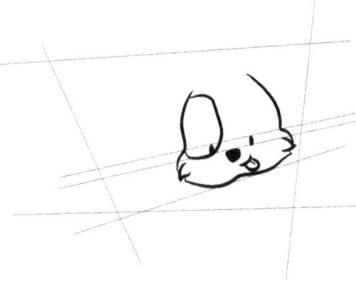
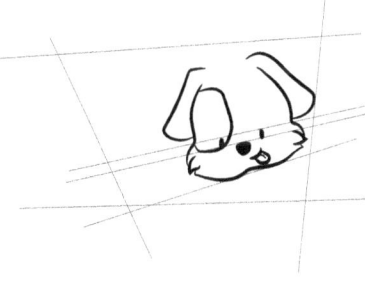

How to draw a dog using a grid. You can download blank grids to practice with in dark and light PDF formats by following the link below.

https://www.lipdf.com/product/grids/

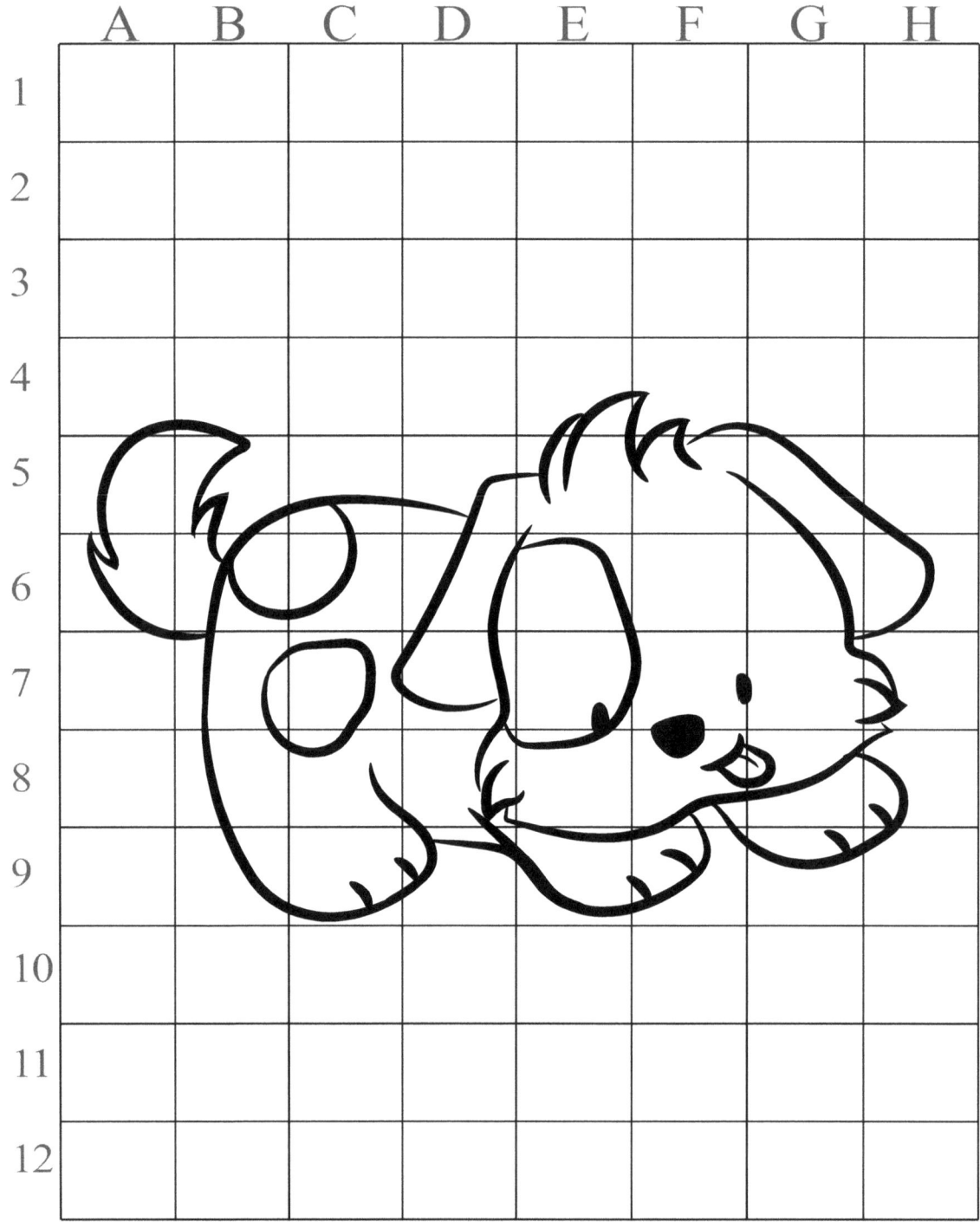

8. Drawing lines on your grid will help you to draw eyes that are focused on a distant object.

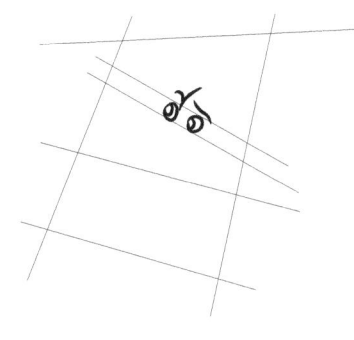
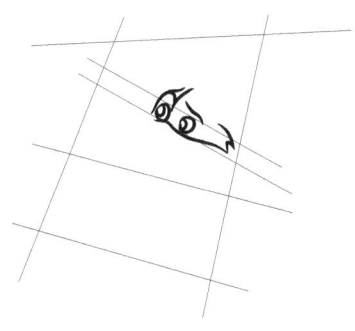
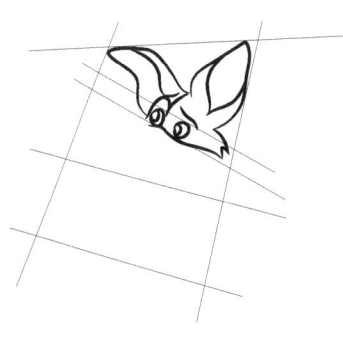

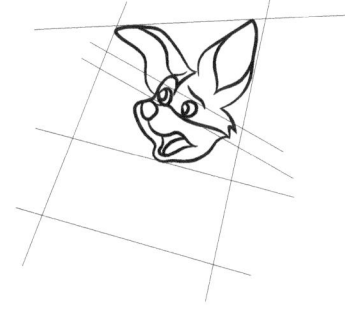
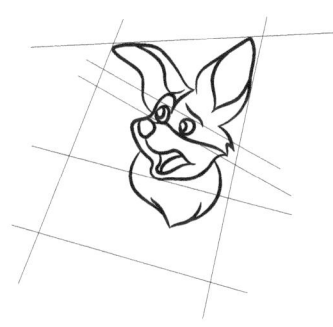
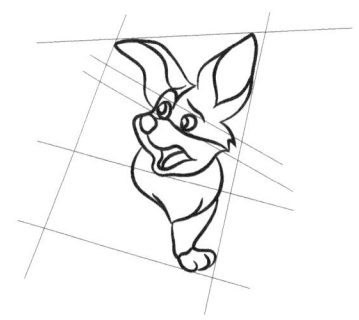

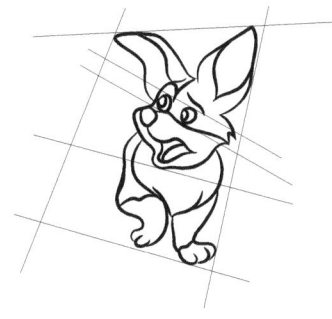

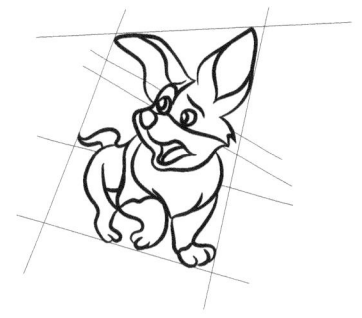

How to draw a dog using a grid. You can download blank grids to practice with in dark and light PDF formats by following the link below.

https://www.lipdf.com/product/grids/

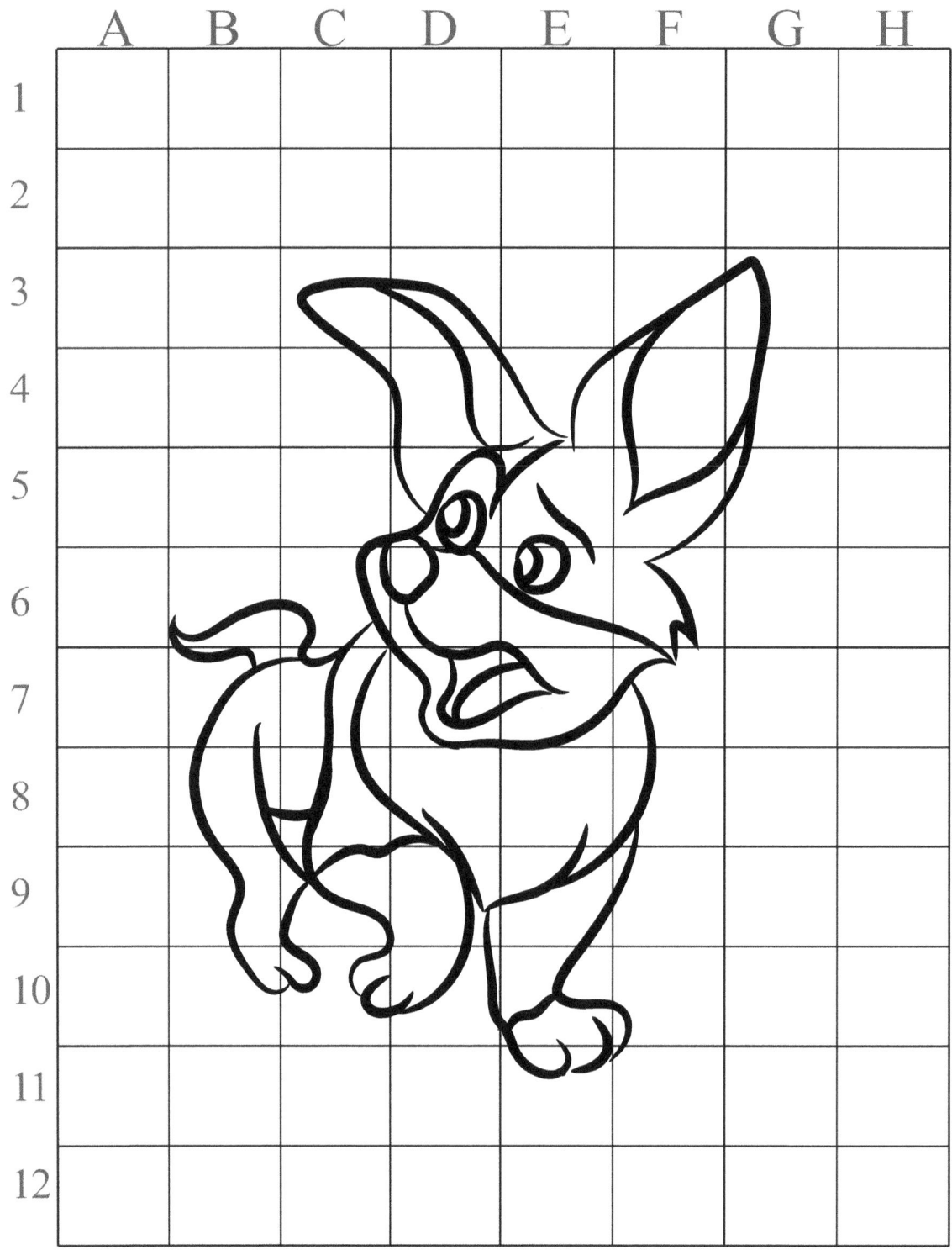

9. Drawing eyes closer together can make the character you are drawing look angrier.

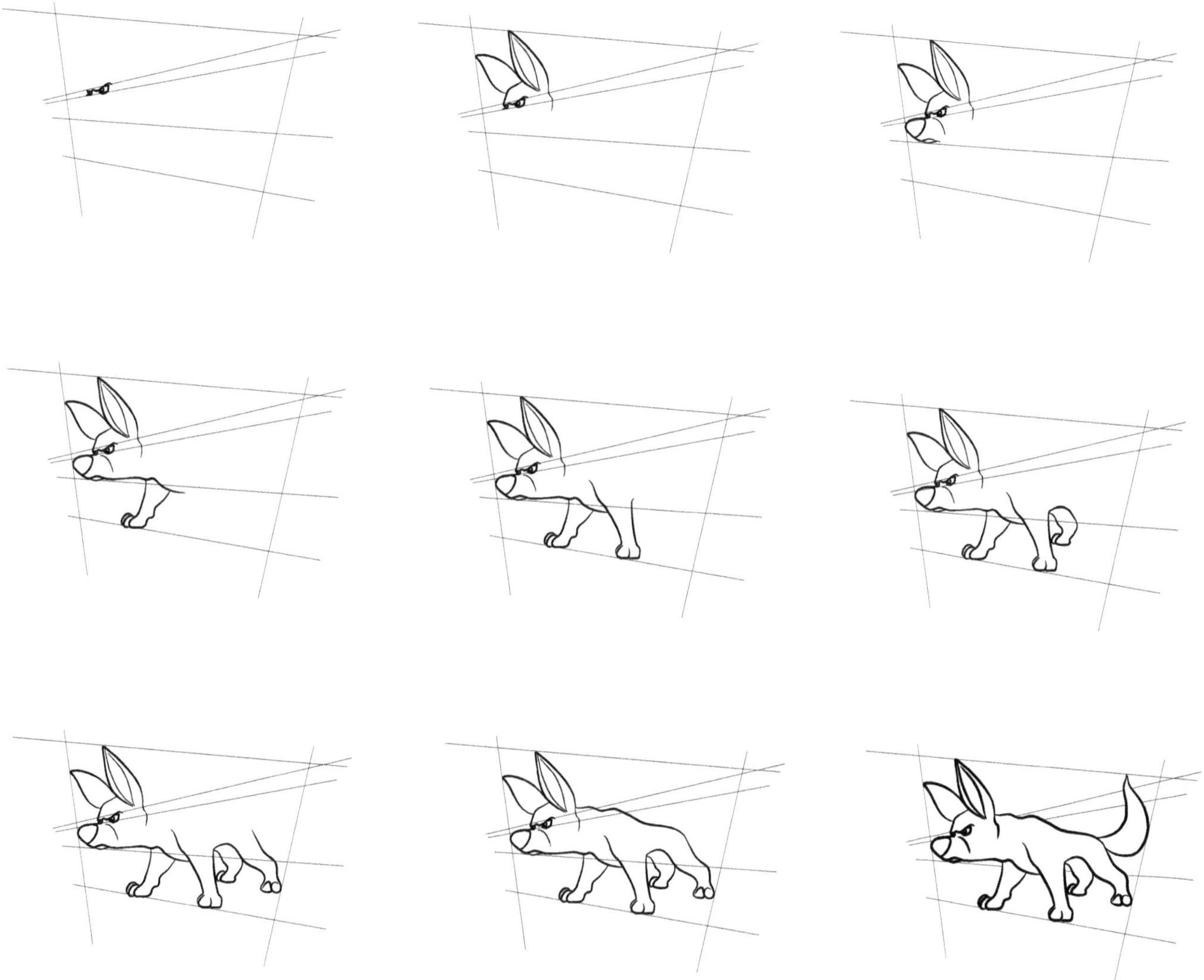

How to draw a dog using a grid. You can download blank grids to practice with in dark and light PDF formats by following the link below.

https://www.lipdf.com/product/grids/

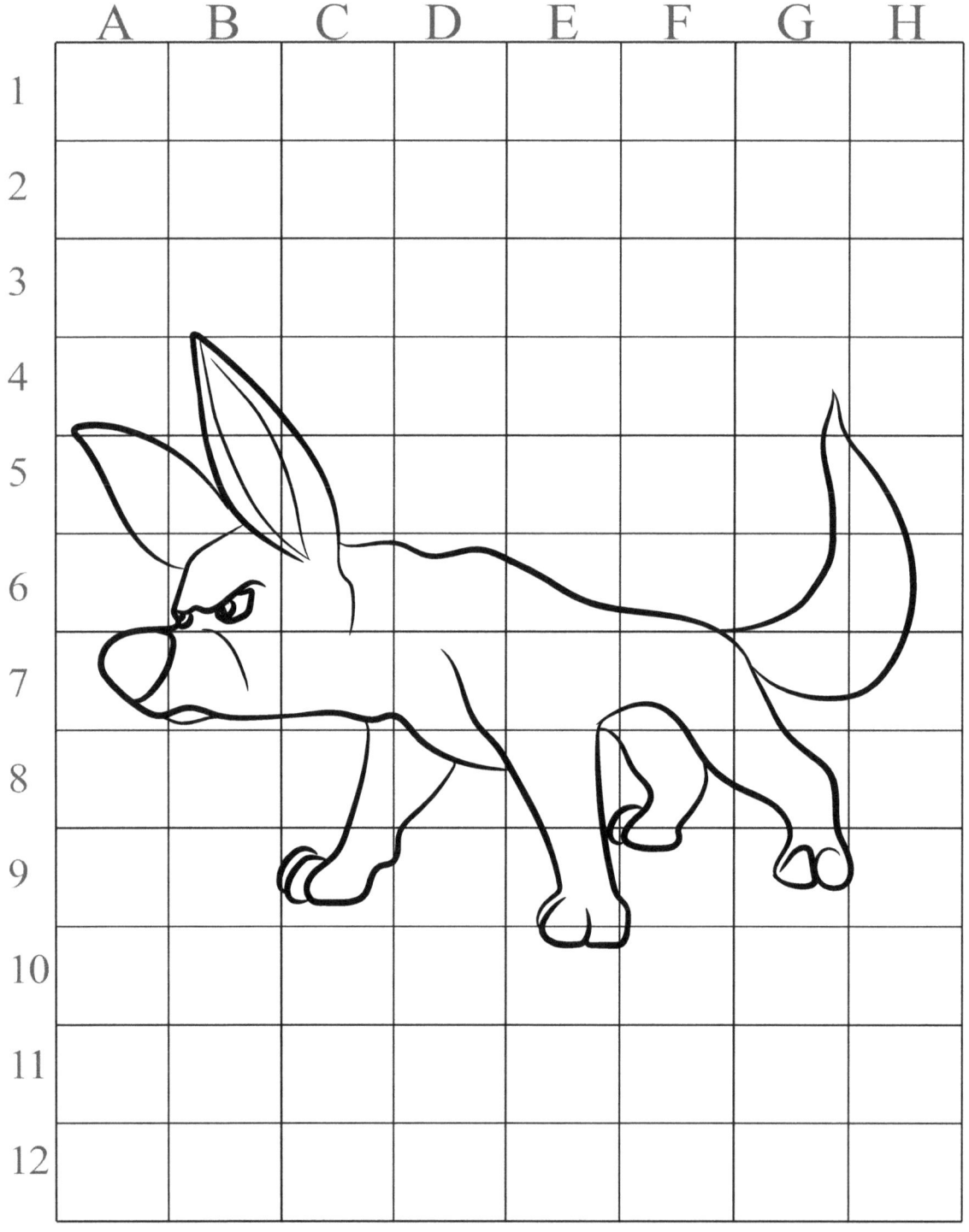

10. Drawing eyes further apart can make your character look more relaxed.

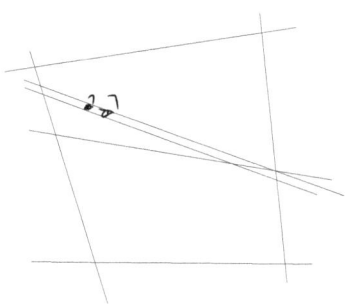 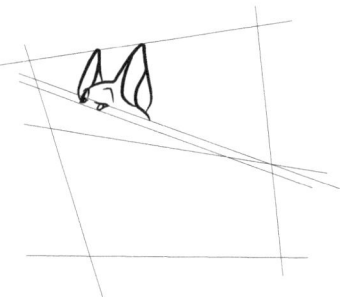 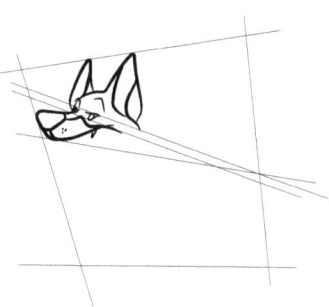

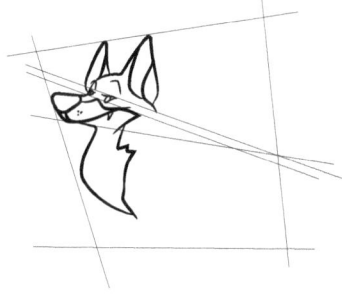 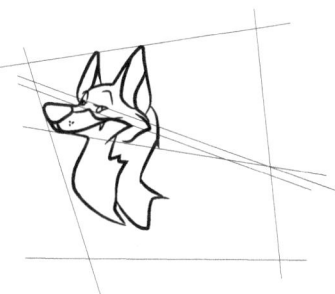 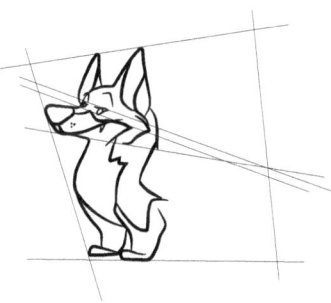

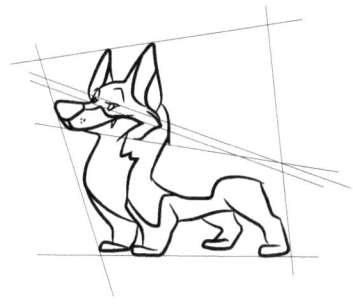 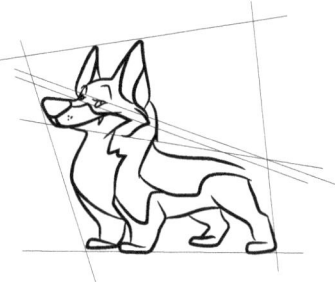 

How to draw a dog using a grid. You can download blank grids to practice with in dark and light PDF formats by following the link below.

https://www.lipdf.com/product/grids/

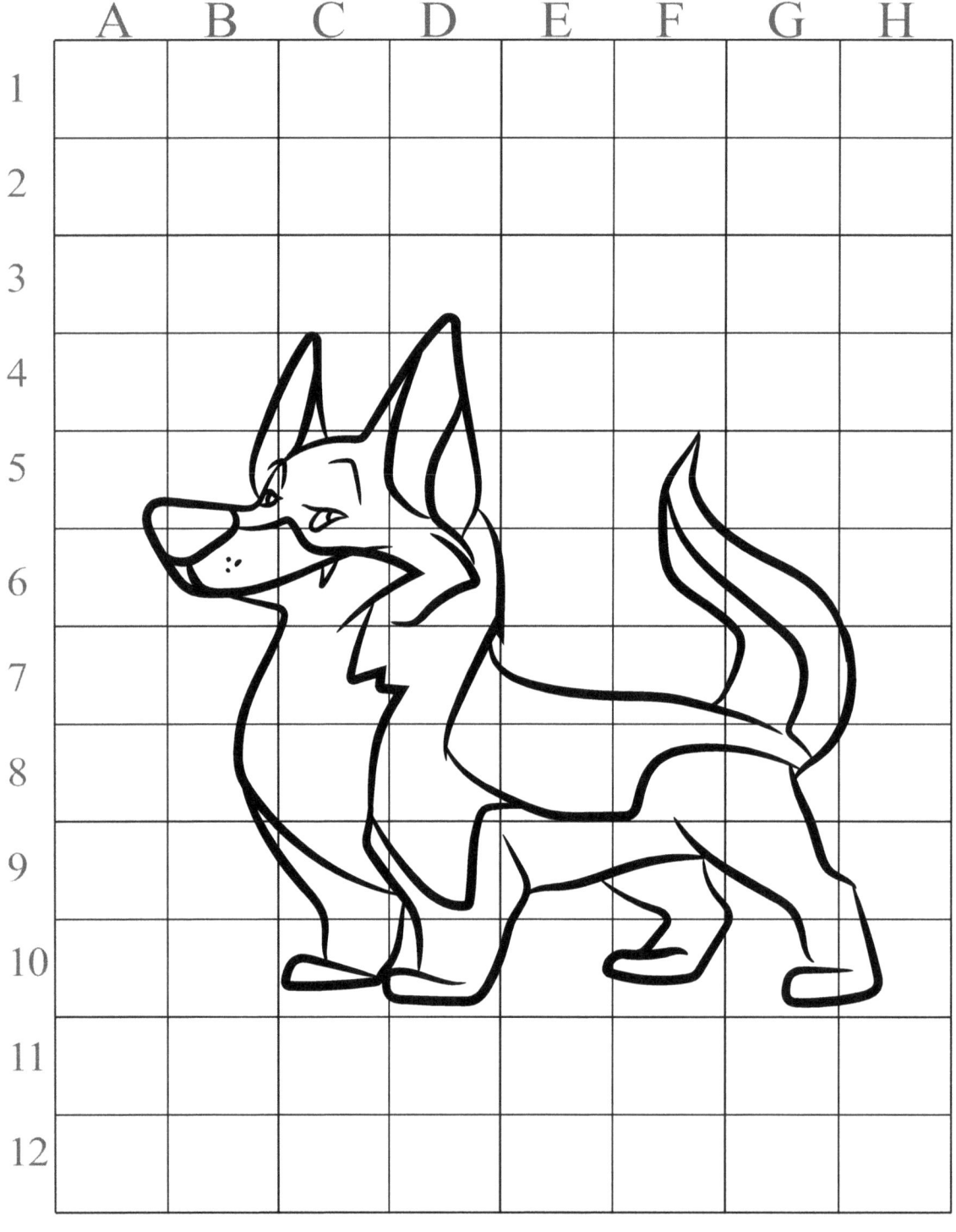

11. You can make your character look surprised or shocked by increasing the distance between the eyes and the eyebrows.

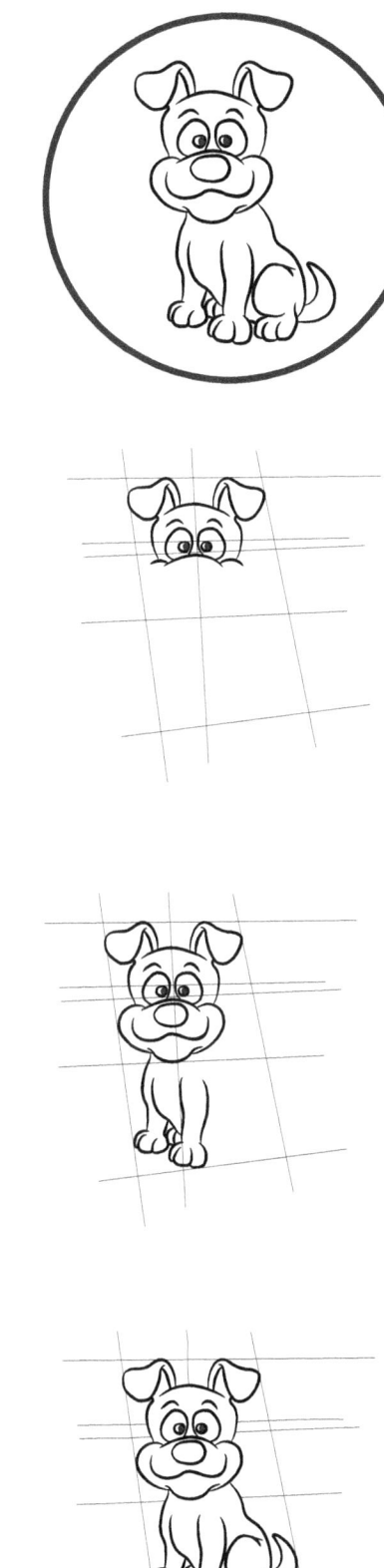

How to draw a dog using a grid. You can download blank grids to practice with in dark and light PDF formats by following the link below.

https://www.lipdf.com/product/grids/

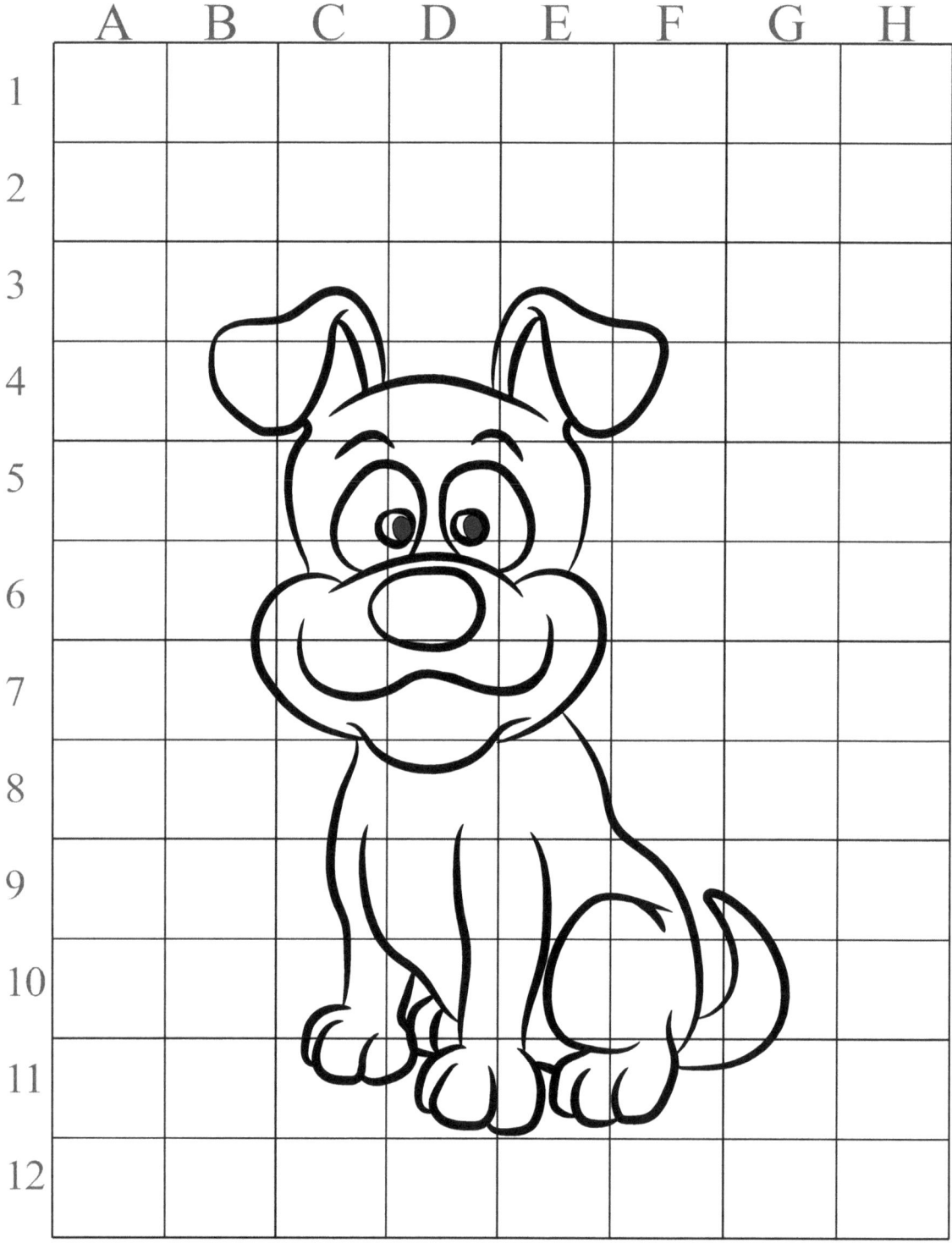

12. The use of ellipses in grids can be very helpful when you want to create round shapes.

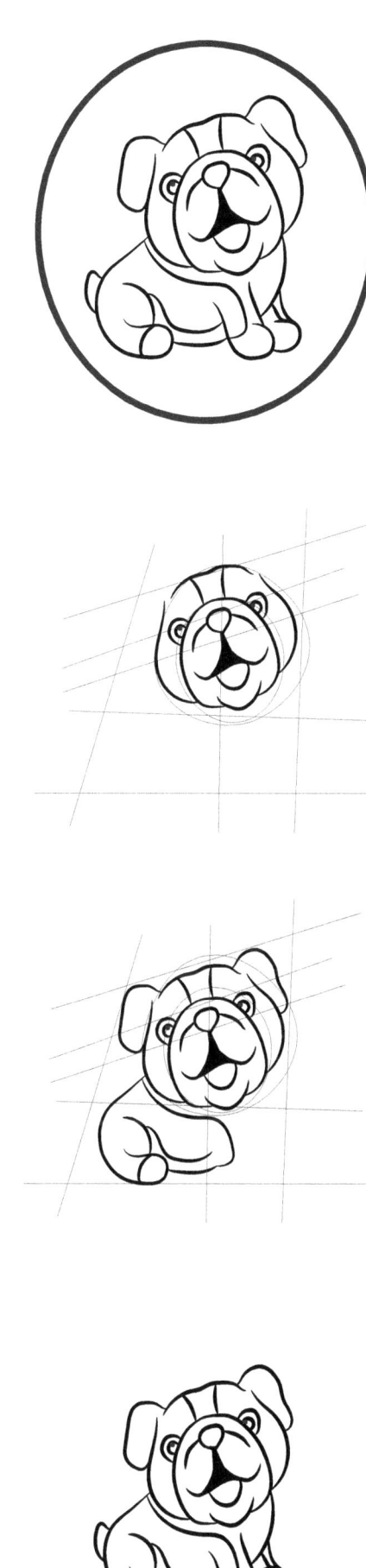

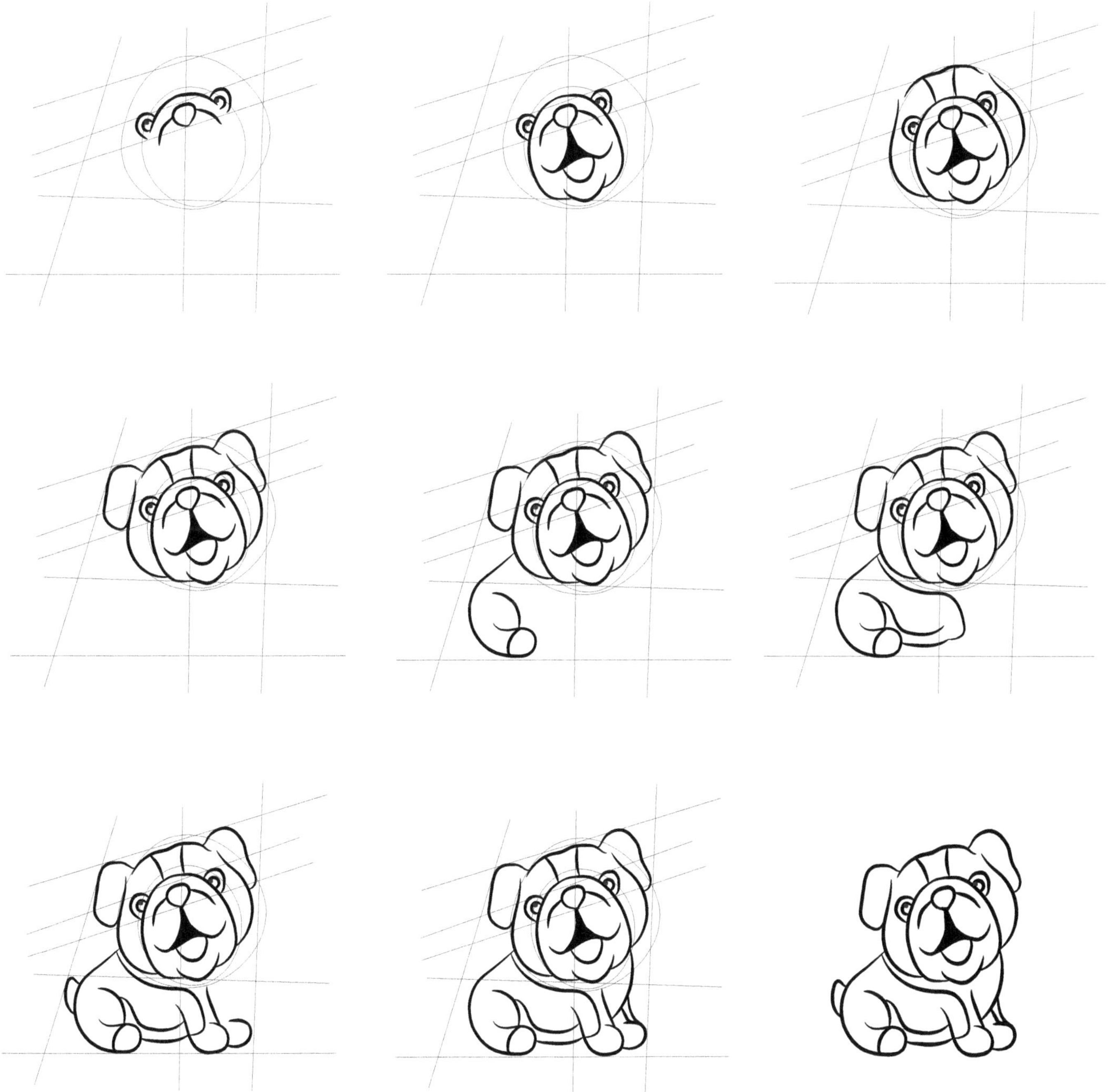

How to draw a dog using a grid. You can download blank grids to practice with in dark and light PDF formats by following the link below.

https://www.lipdf.com/product/grids/

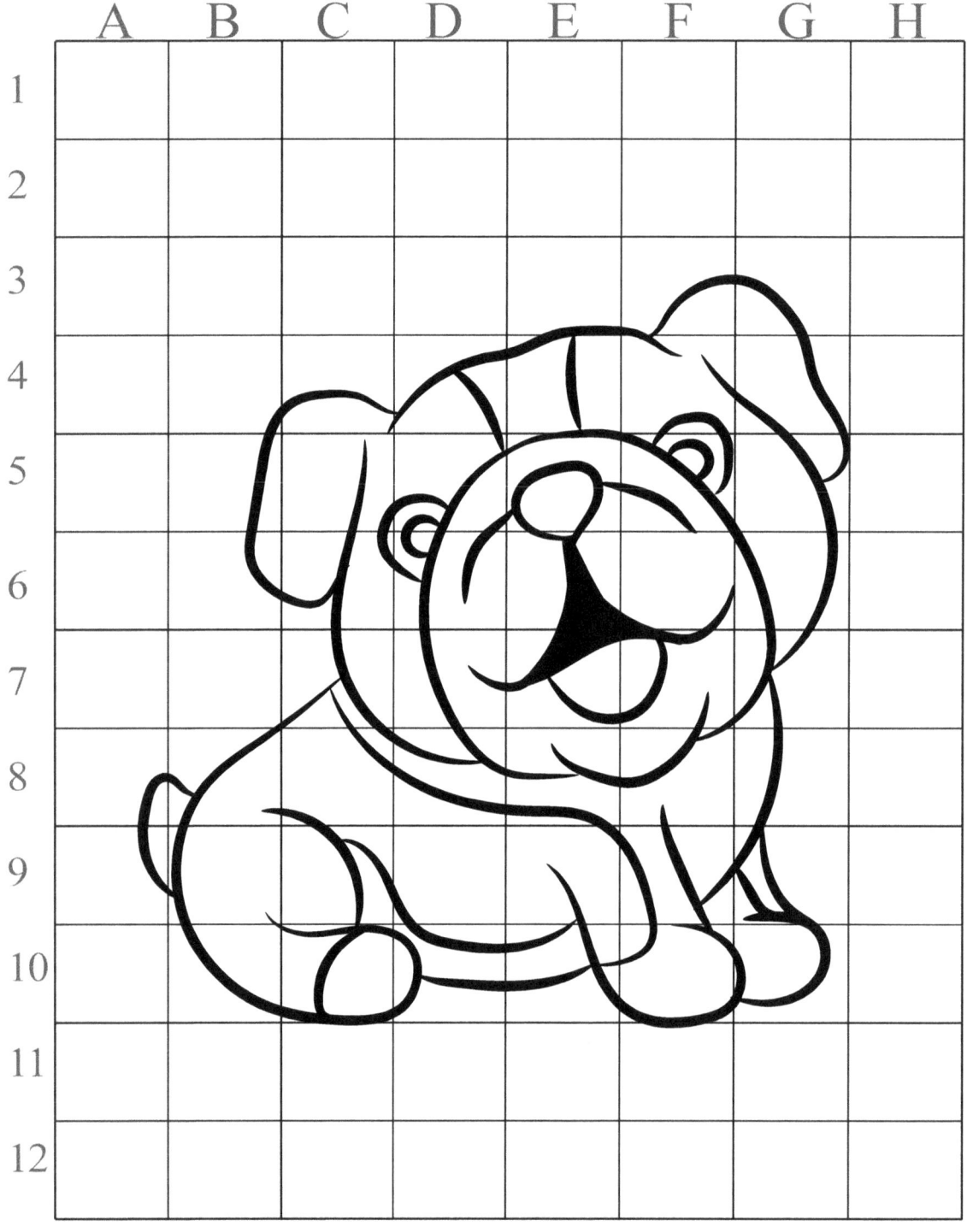

13. A surprised look can be created by raising the eyebrows and opening the mouth.

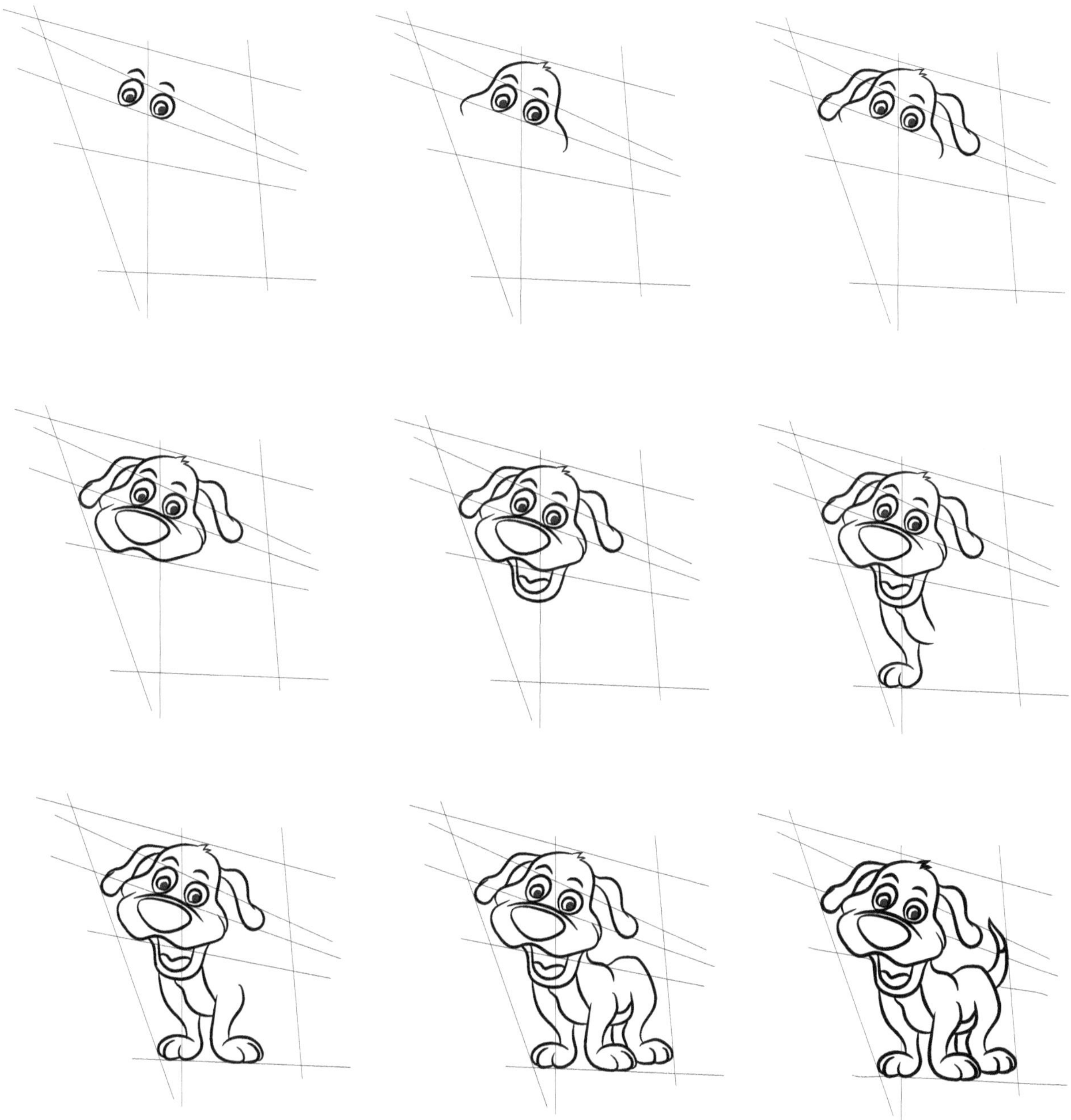

How to draw a dog using a grid. You can download blank grids to practice with in dark and light PDF formats by following the link below.

https://www.lipdf.com/product/grids/

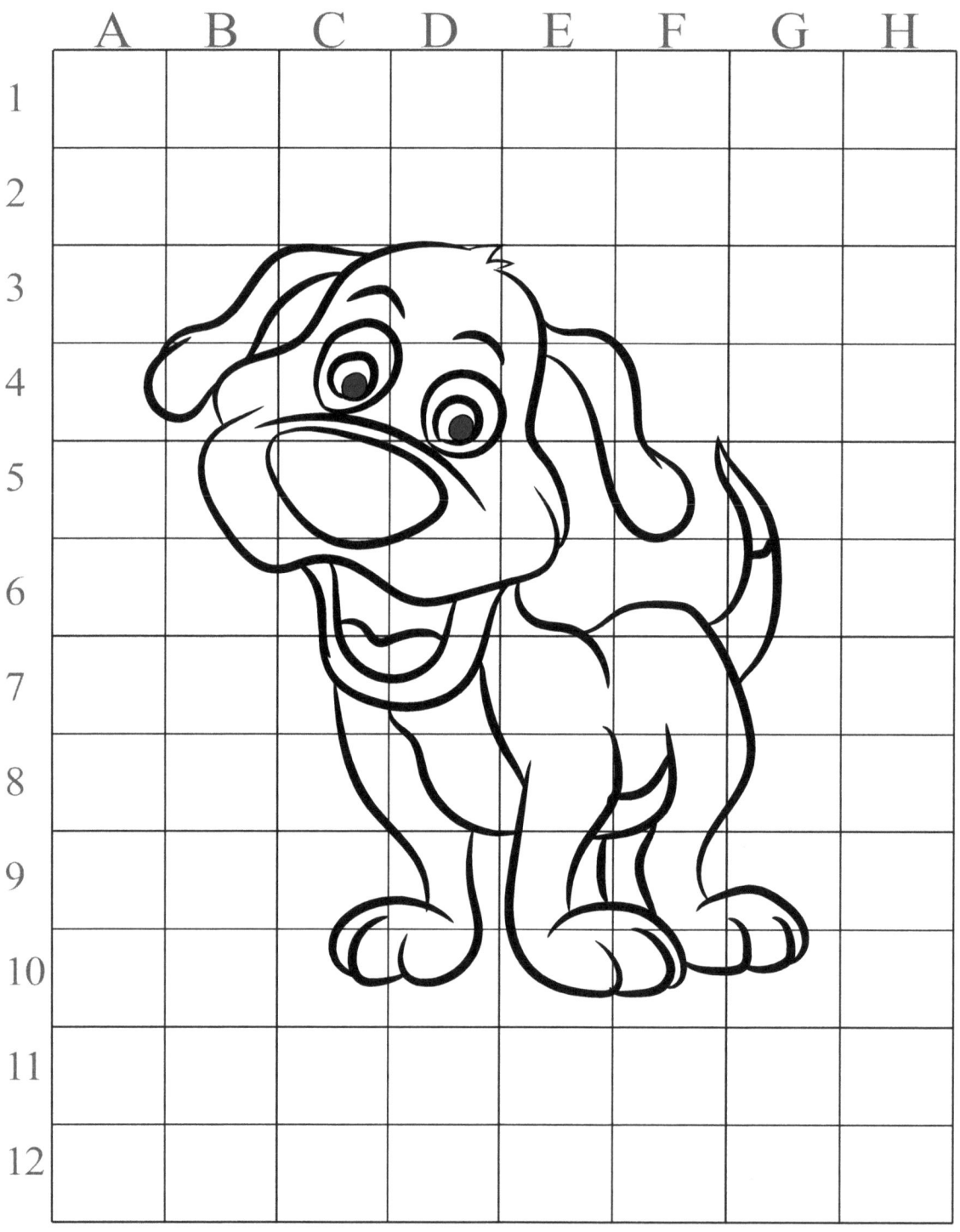

14. Separate your grid into sections to help you decide how you want to proportion your drawing. This can help you to alter the height of your character.

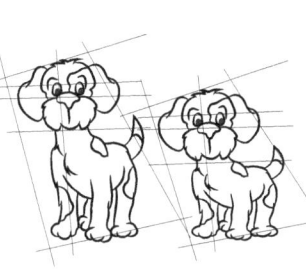

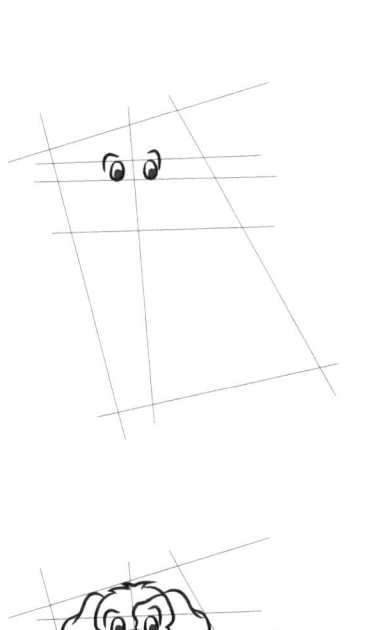
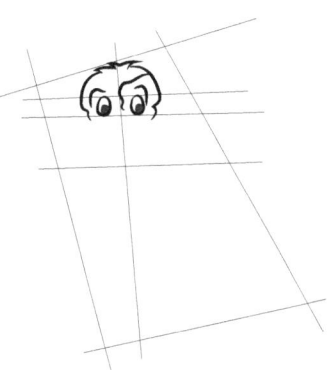
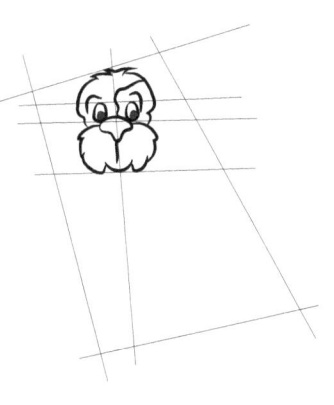
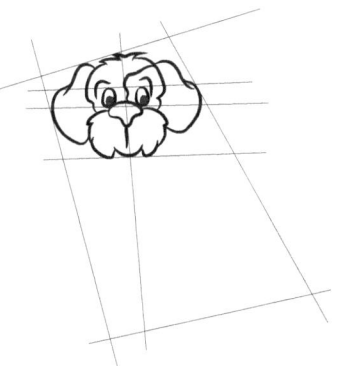
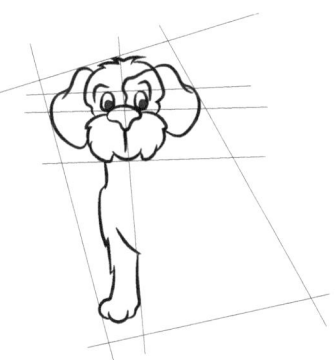
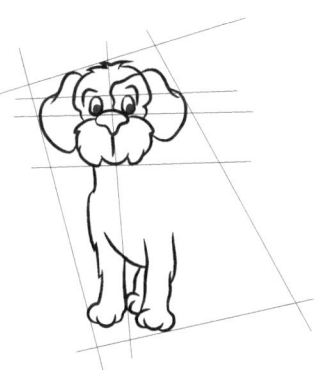

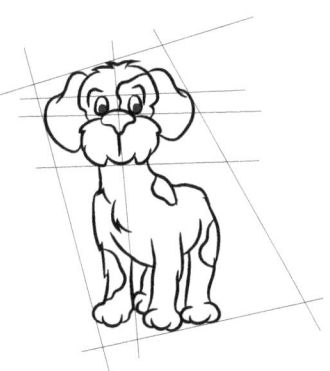

How to draw a dog using a grid. You can download blank grids to practice with in dark and light PDF formats by following the link below.

https://www.lipdf.com/product/grids/

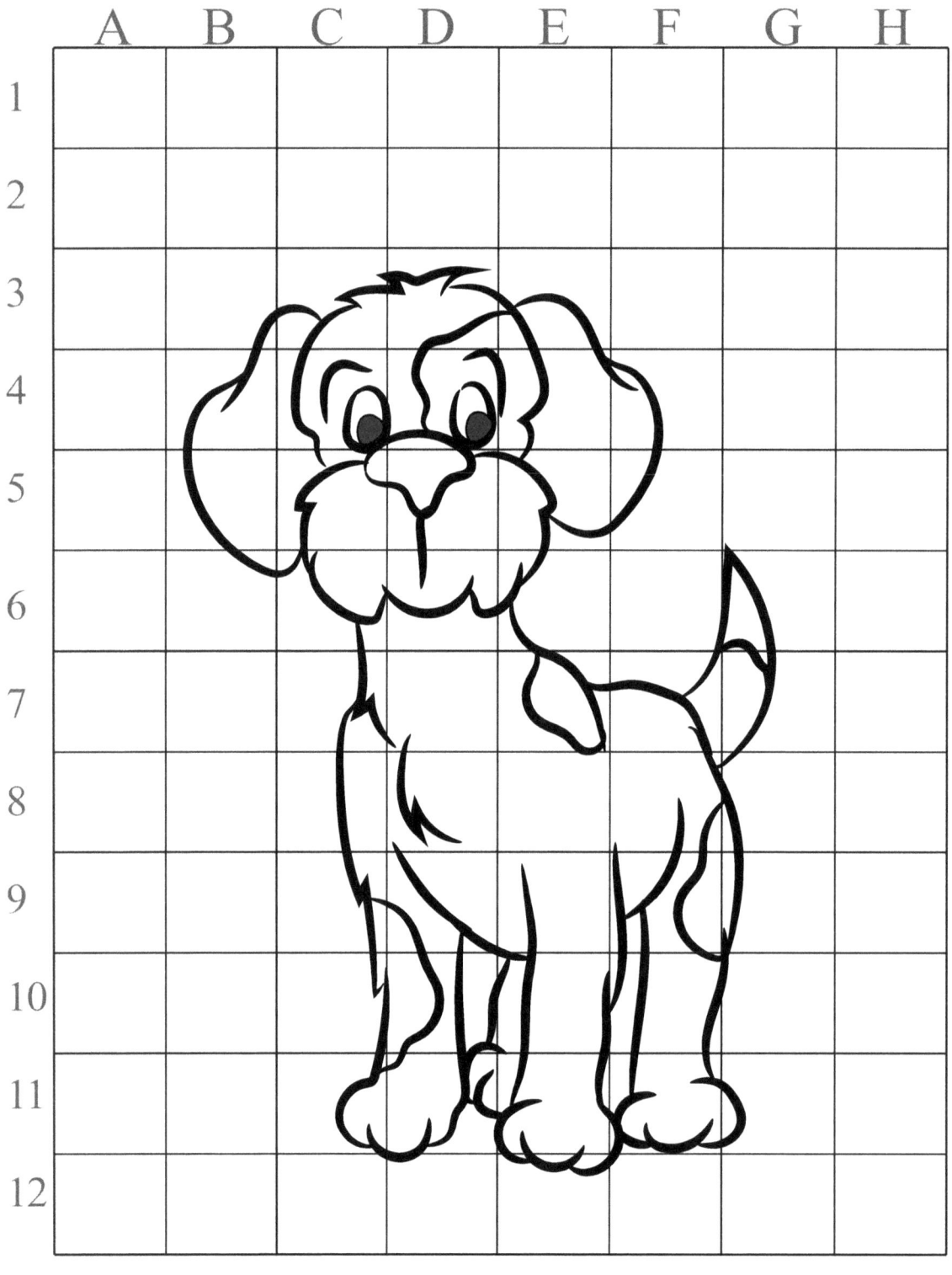

15. Starting your drawing with the eyes will help your initial sketch to take shape. Follow that by constructing the head.

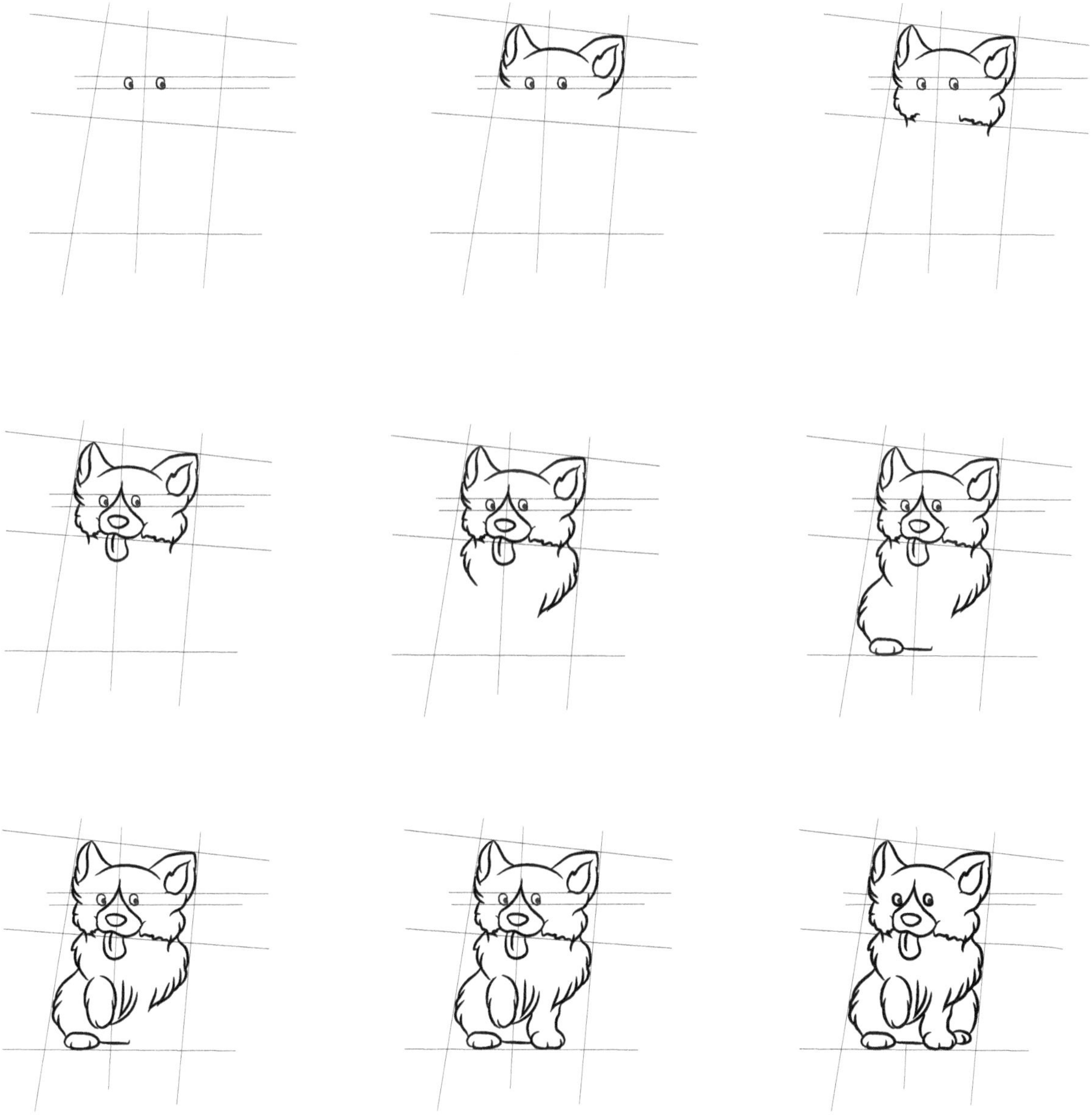

How to draw a dog using a grid. You can download blank grids to practice with in dark and light PDF formats by following the link below.

https://www.lipdf.com/product/grids/

16. Even very small changes in your drawing can affect the emotion that your character is expressing.

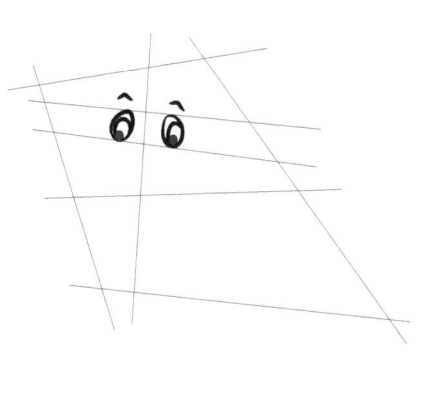

How to draw a dog using a grid. You can download blank grids to practice with in dark and light PDF formats by following the link below.

https://www.lipdf.com/product/grids/

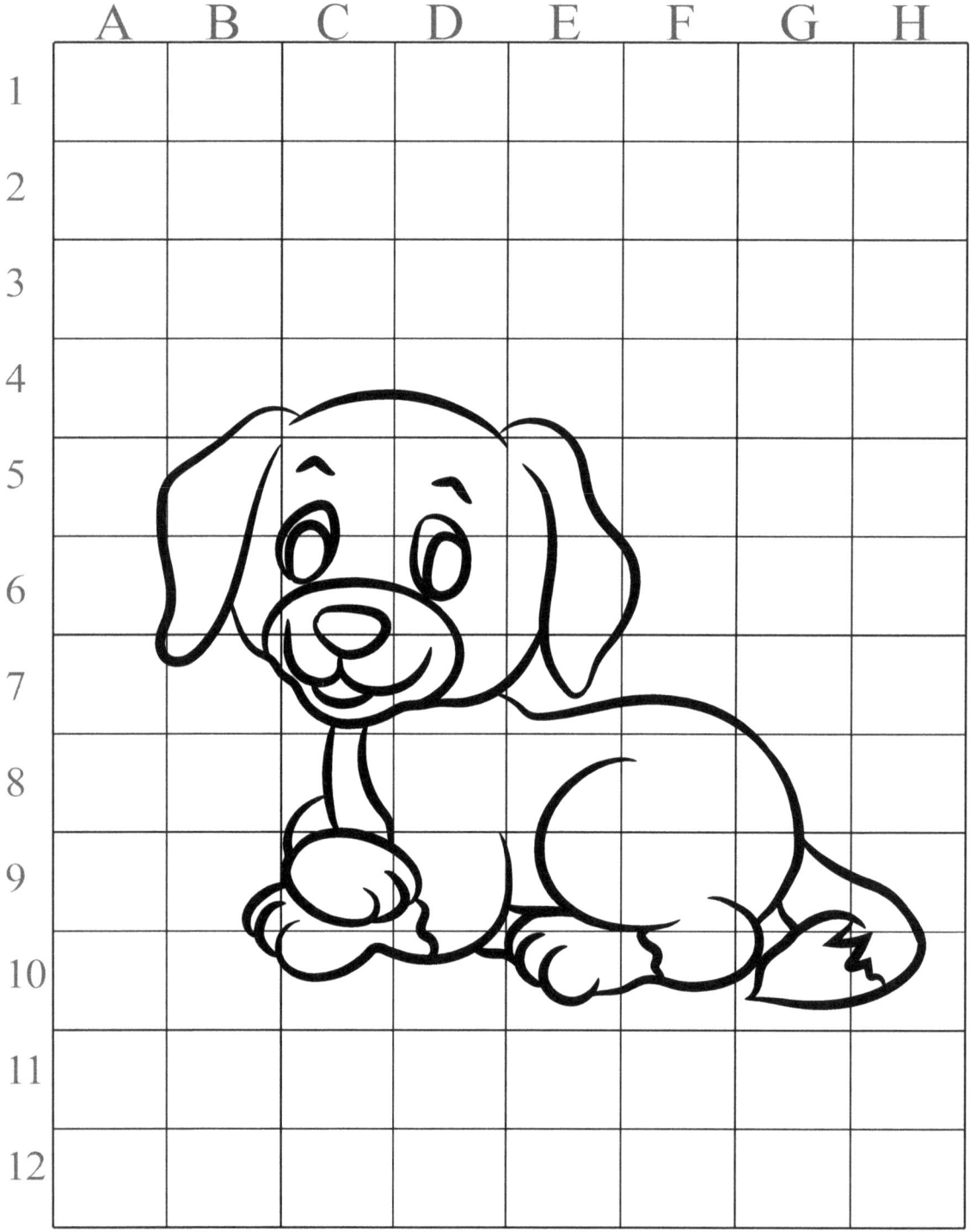

17. Changing the position of your characters eyebrows can slightly alter emotional expression.

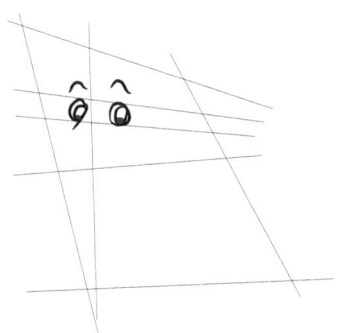
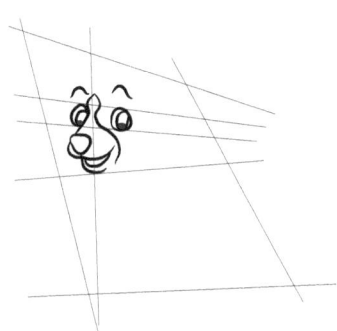
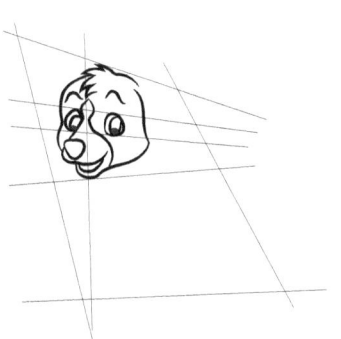

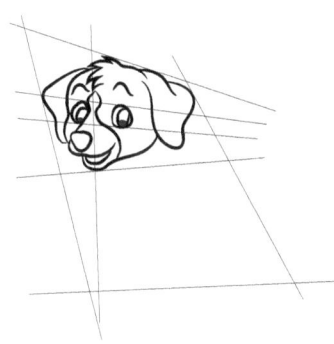

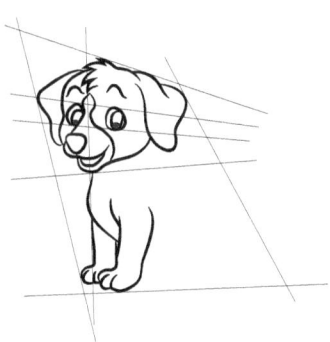

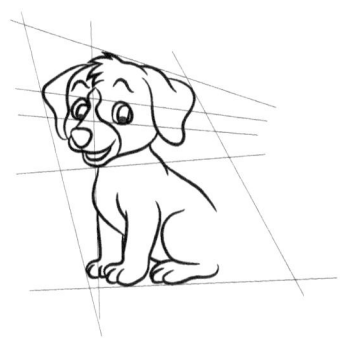

How to draw a dog using a grid. You can download blank grids to practice with in dark and light PDF formats by following the link below.

https://www.lipdf.com/product/grids/

18. The way that you draw lines on your grid can help you to draw eyes that are focused on a distant object.

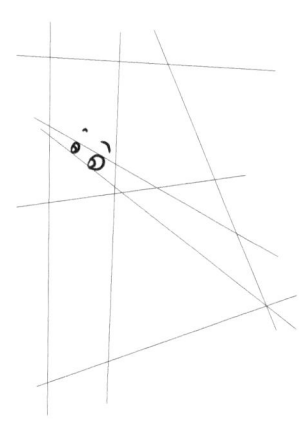
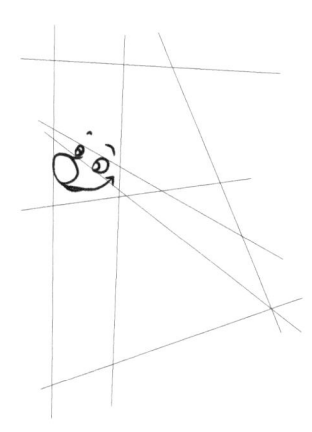
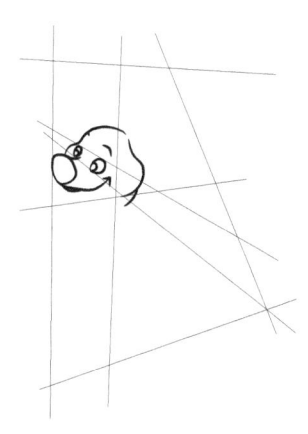
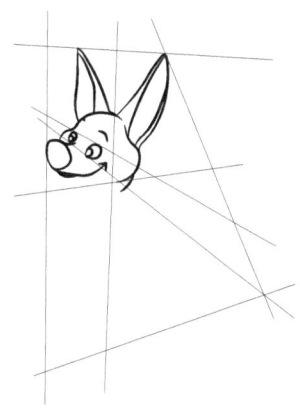
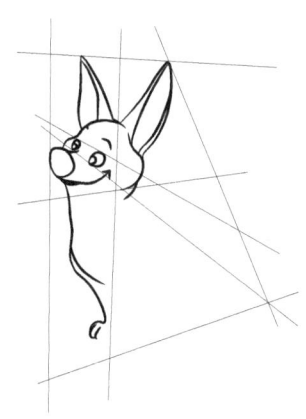
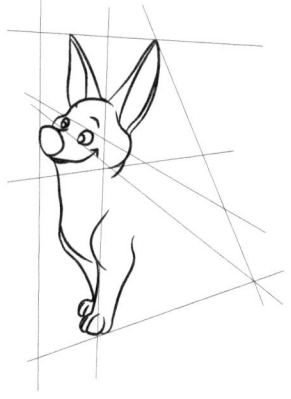
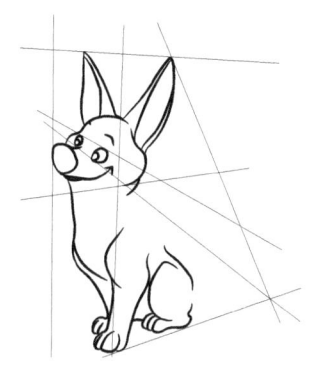
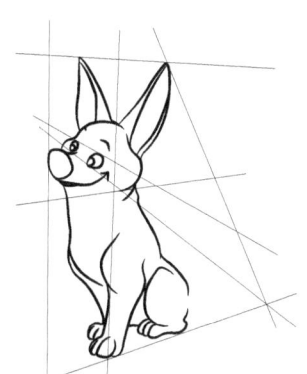

How to draw a dog using a grid. You can download blank grids to practice with in dark and light PDF formats by following the link below.

https://www.lipdf.com/product/grids/

19. You can turn your character's head while keeping the position of its body the same.

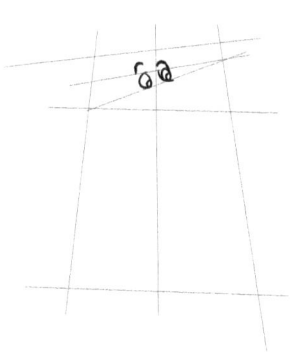
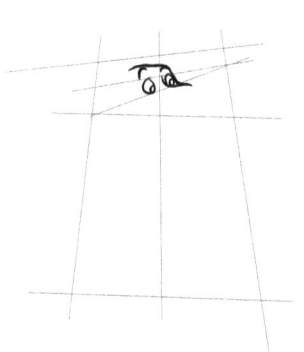
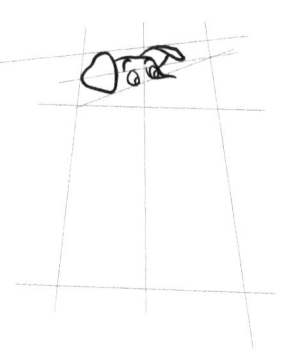

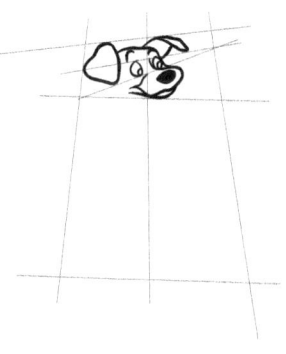

How to draw a dog using a grid. You can download blank grids to practice with in dark and light PDF formats by following the link below.

https://www.lipdf.com/product/grids/

20. After you have drawn your character's head it is easier to add small details.

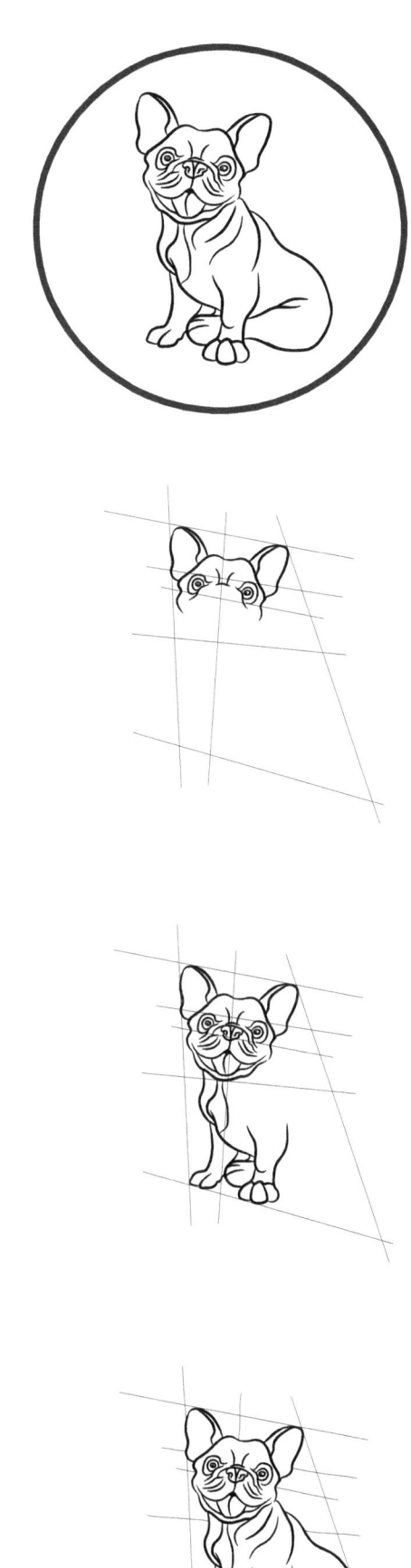

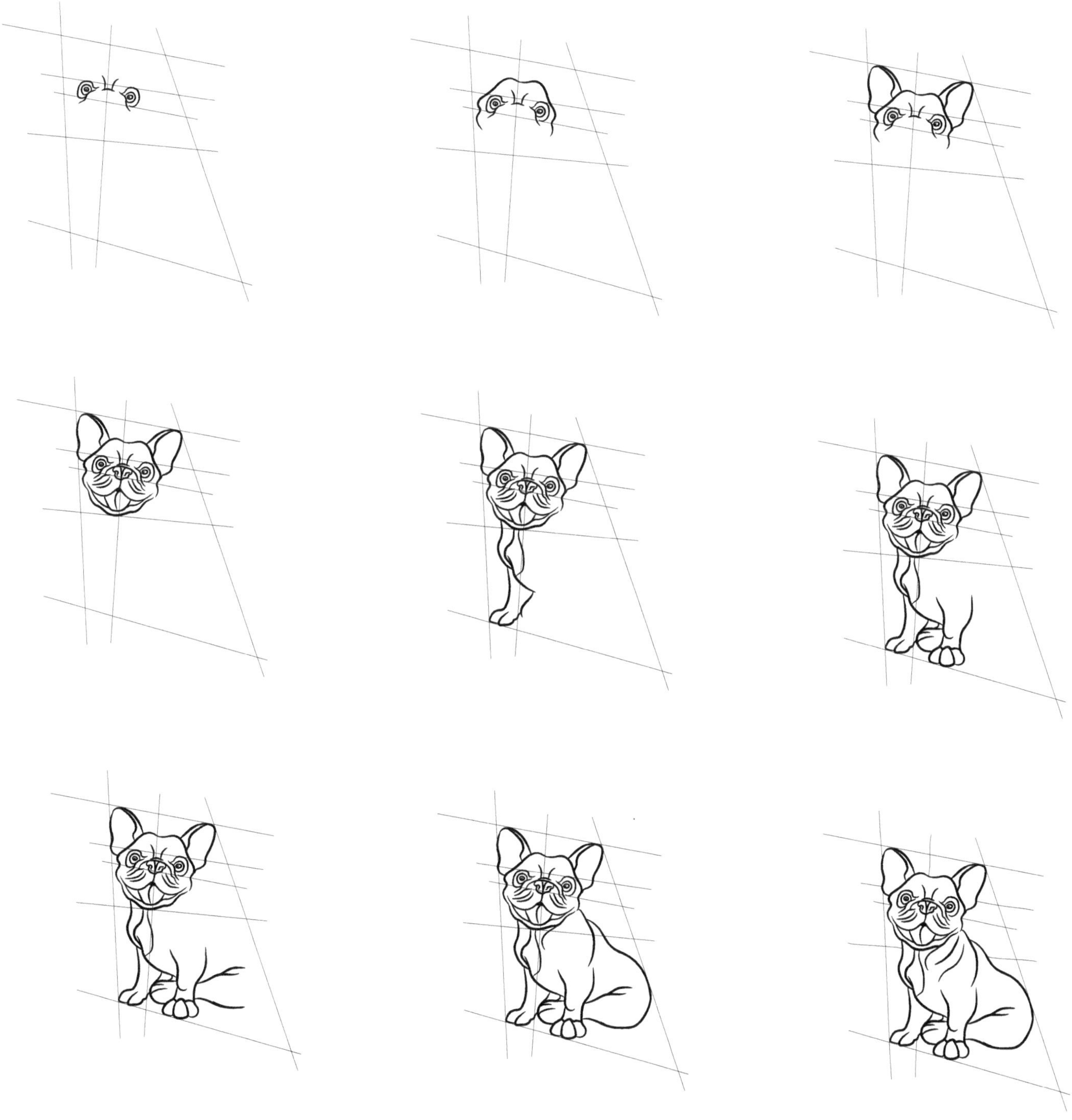

How to draw a dog using a grid. You can download blank grids to practice with in dark and light PDF formats by following the link below.

https://www.lipdf.com/product/grids/

21. Sometimes minor changes in your drawing can make the situation look very different.

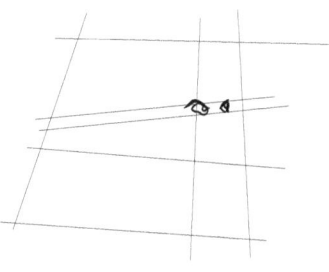
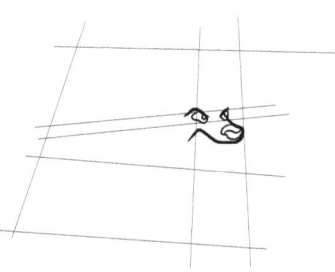
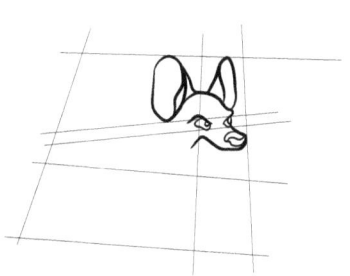

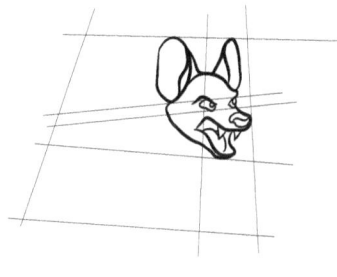
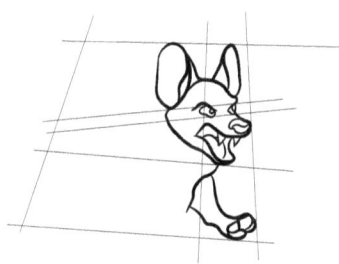
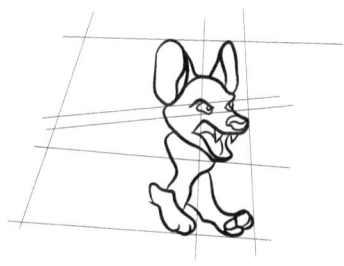

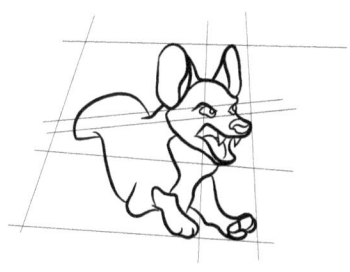

How to draw a dog using a grid. You can download blank grids to practice with in dark and light PDF formats by following the link below.

https://www.lipdf.com/product/grids/

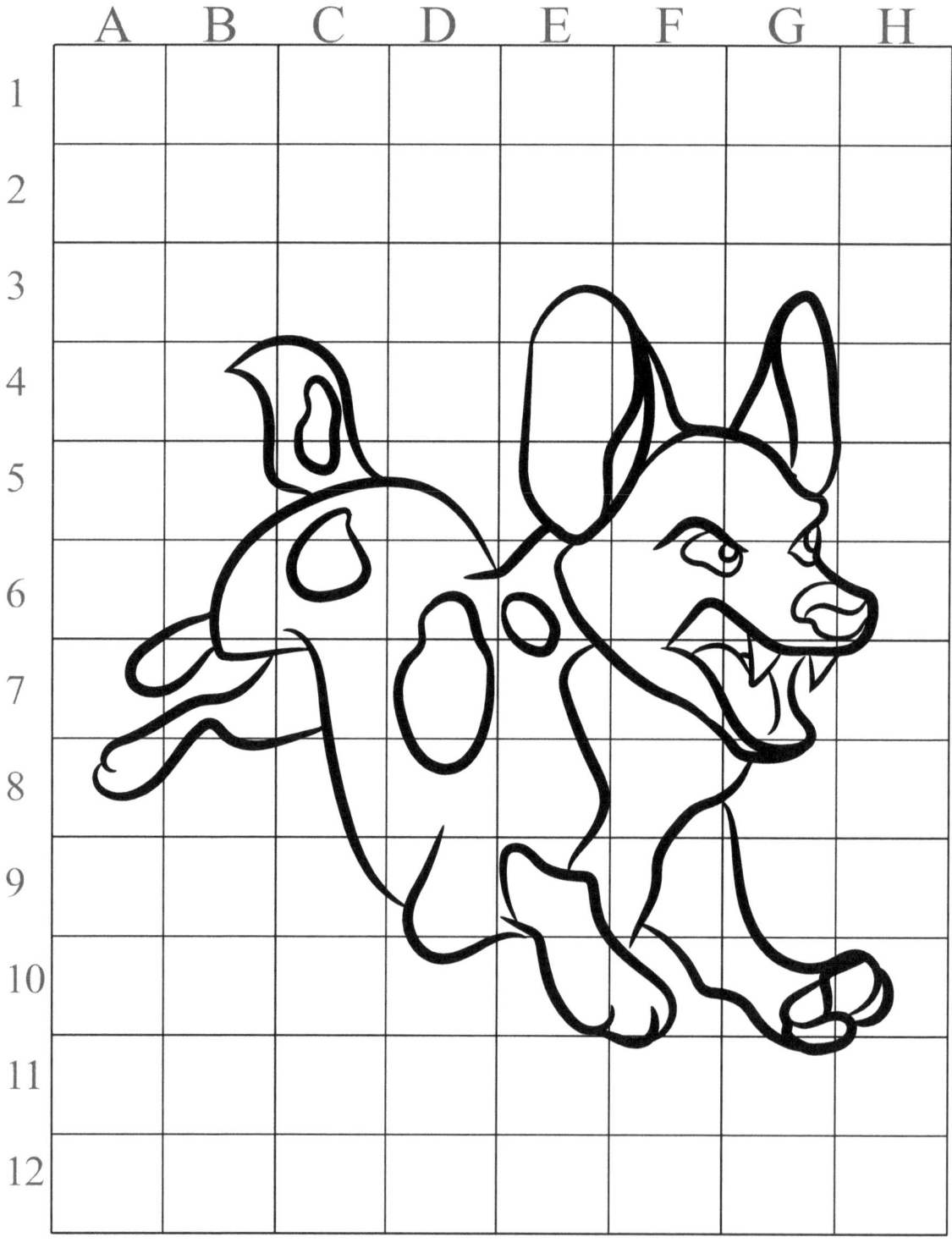

22. Moving around your character's pupils can alter the behaviour of the character from looking at something to thinking about something.

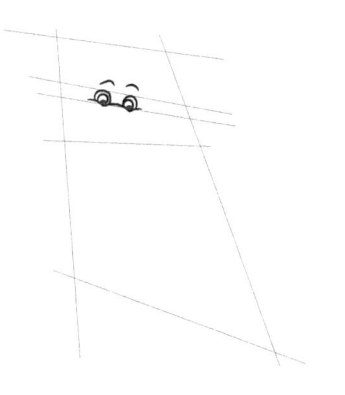
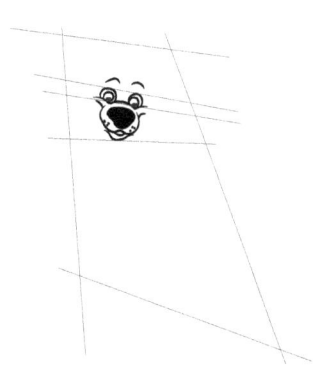
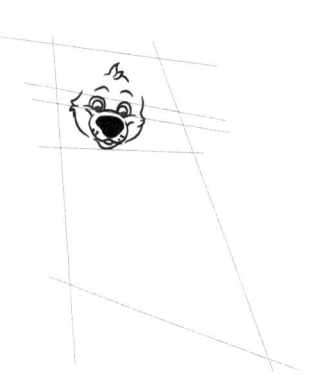

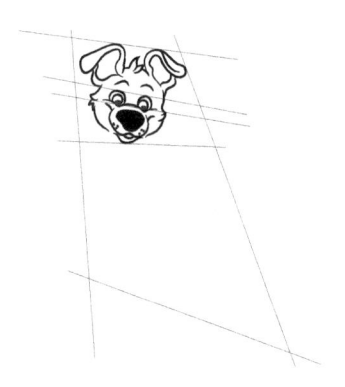

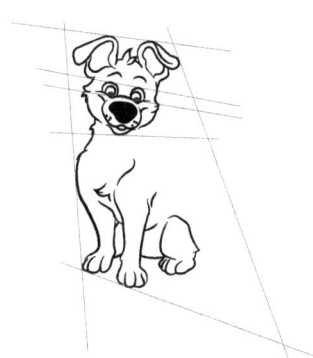

How to draw a dog using a grid. You can download blank grids to practice with in dark and light PDF formats by following the link below.

https://www.lipdf.com/product/grids/

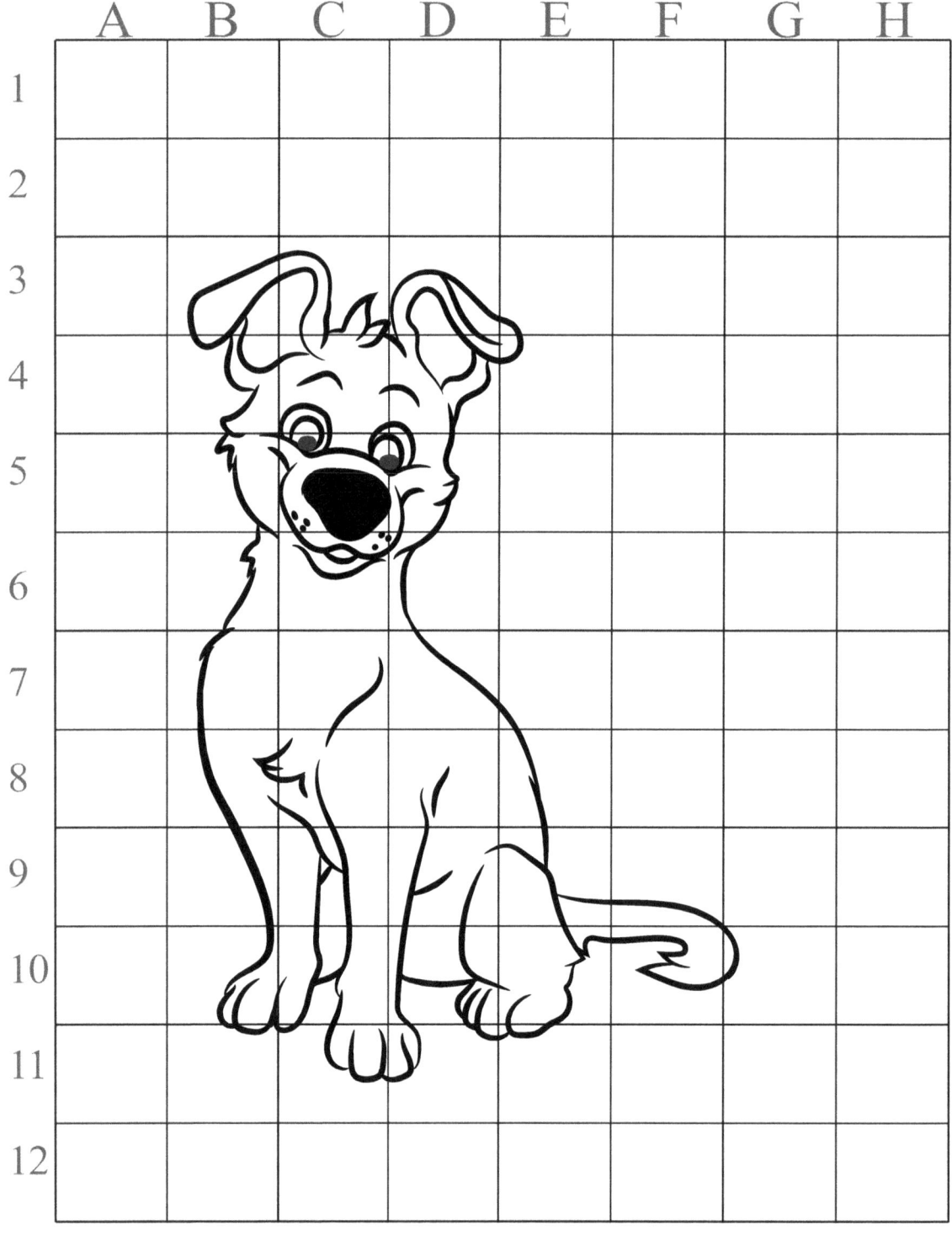

23. Separate your grid into sections to help you decide how you want to proportion your drawing. This can help you to alter the height of your character.

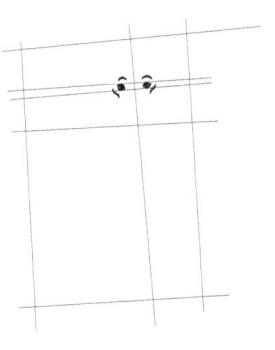

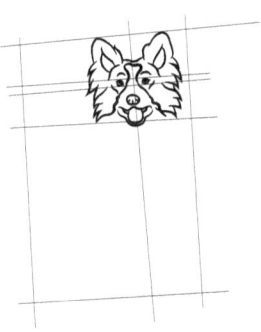

How to draw a dog using a grid. You can download blank grids to practice with in dark and light PDF formats by following the link below.

https://www.lipdf.com/product/grids/

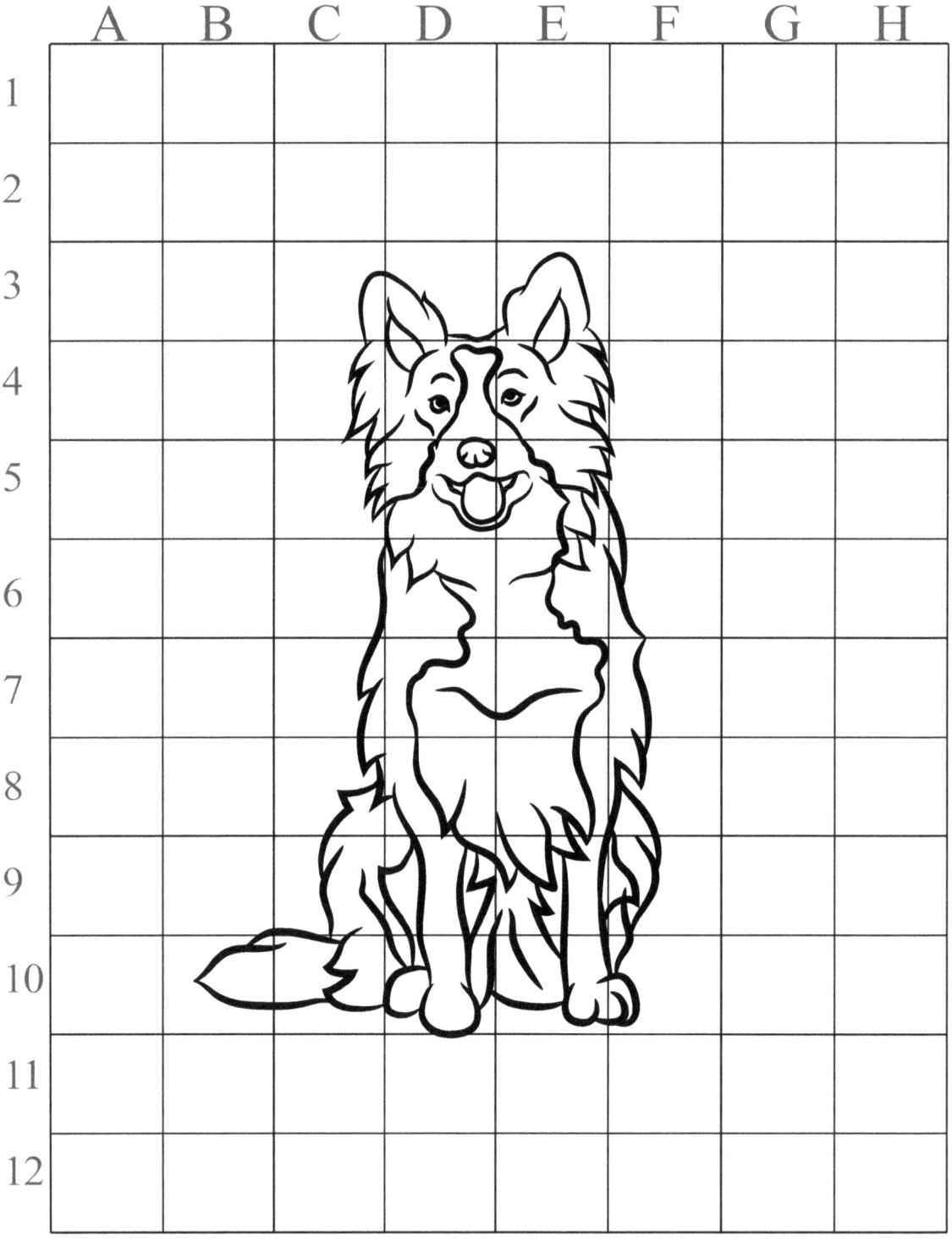

24. Starting your drawing with the eyes will help your initial sketch to take shape.

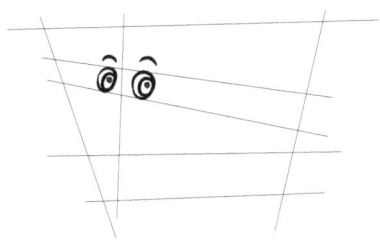 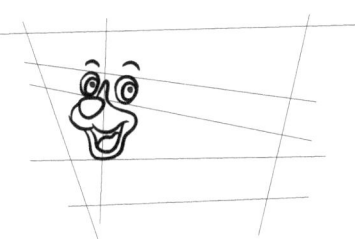 

  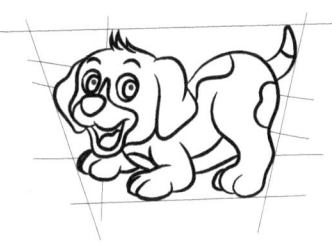

How to draw a dog using a grid. You can download blank grids to practice with in dark and light PDF formats by following the link below.

https://www.lipdf.com/product/grids/

25. You can change your character's features by making small adjustments.

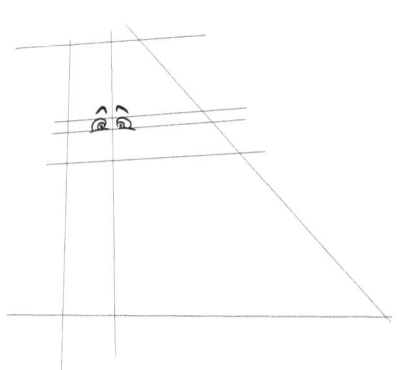
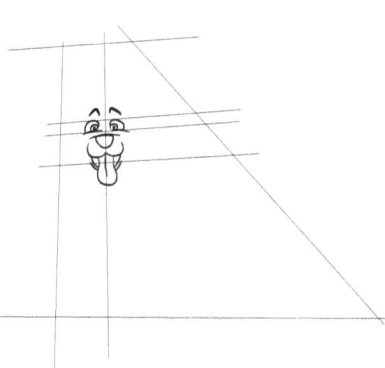
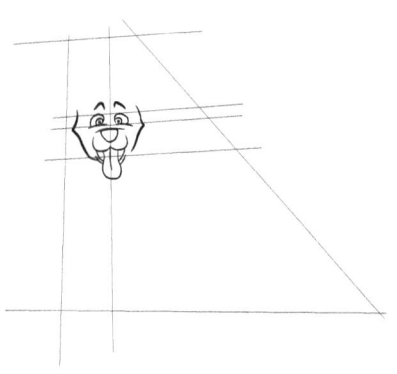

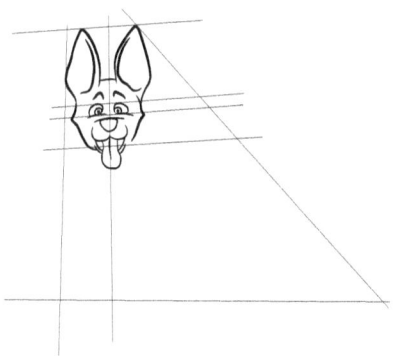

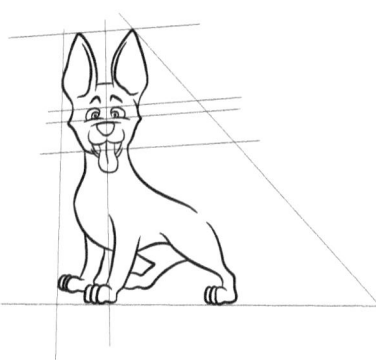
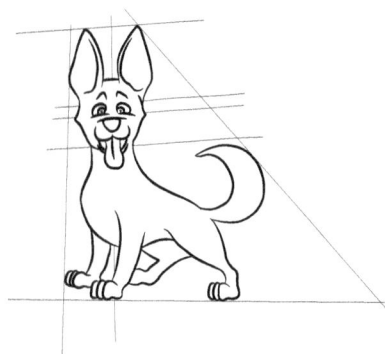

How to draw a dog using a grid. You can download blank grids to practice with in dark and light PDF formats by following the link below.

https://www.lipdf.com/product/grids/

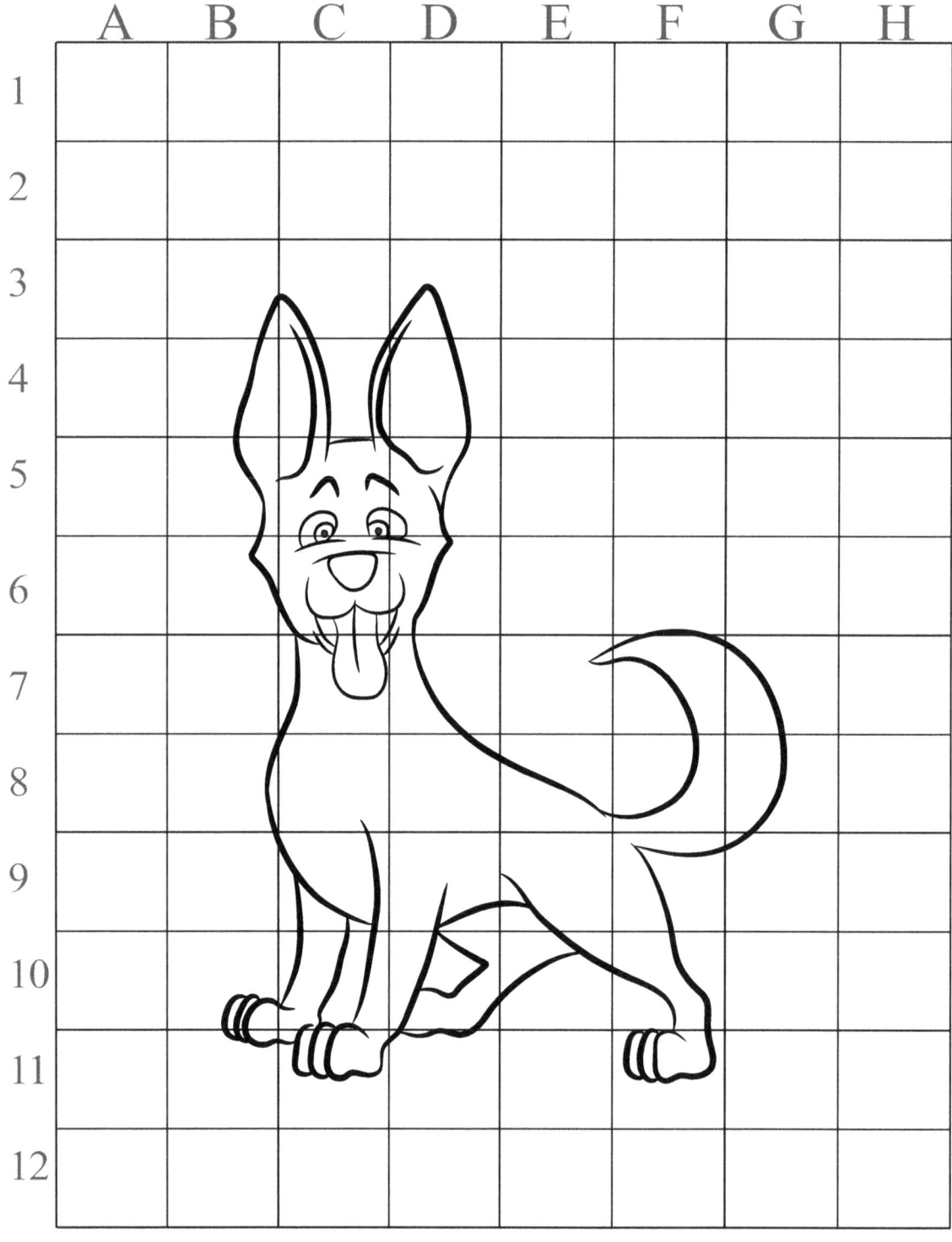

26. The use of overlapping ellipses in grids can be very helpful when you want to create round shapes.

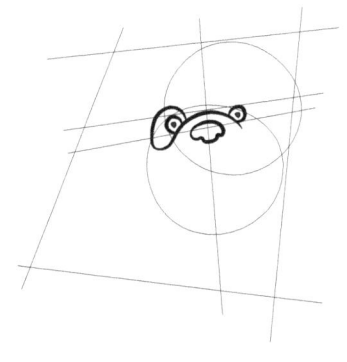 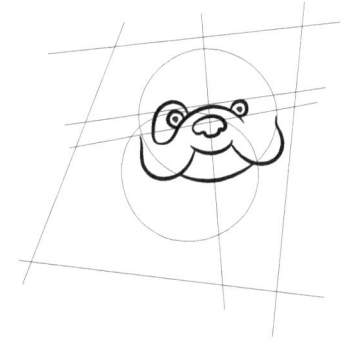 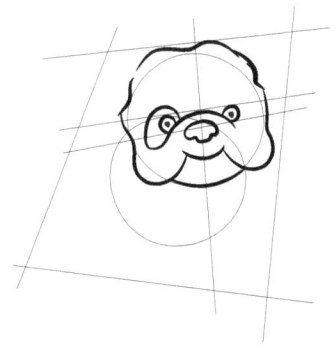

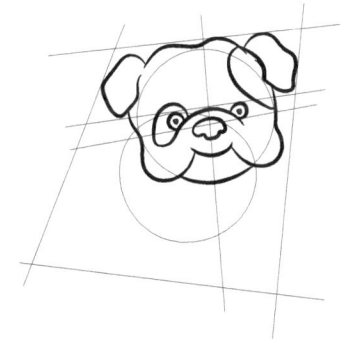 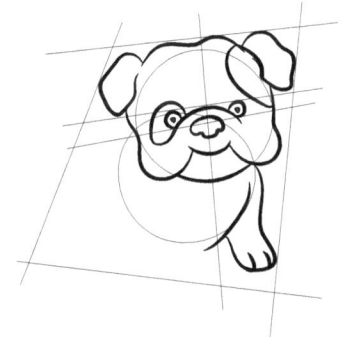 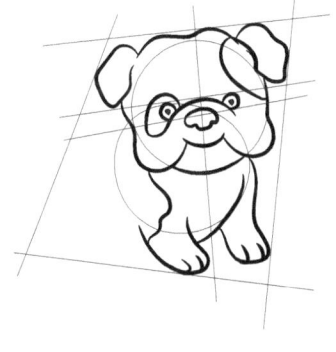

How to draw a dog using a grid. You can download blank grids to practice with in dark and light PDF formats by following the link below.

https://www.lipdf.com/product/grids/

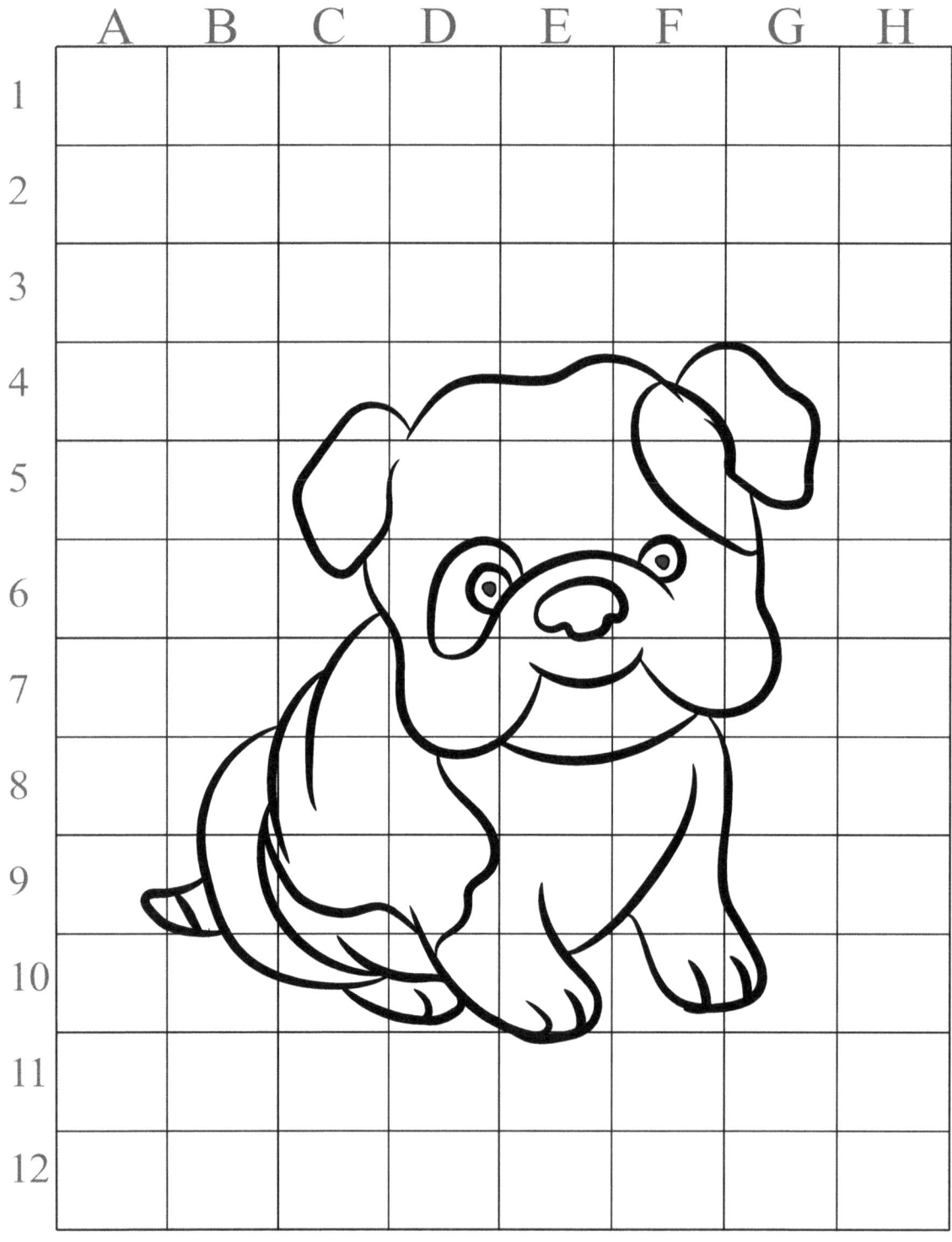

27. Drawing lines on your grid will help you to draw eyes that are focused on a distant object.

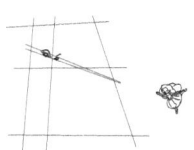

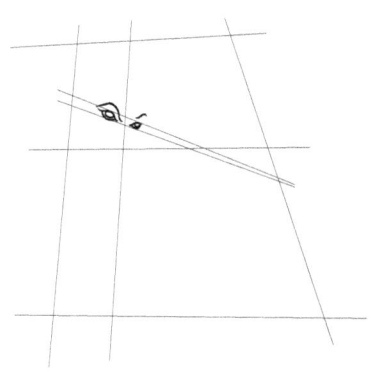
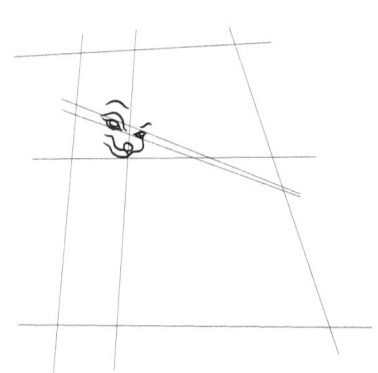
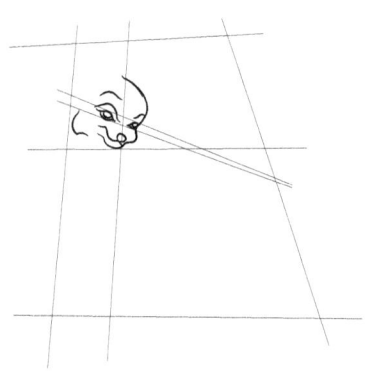

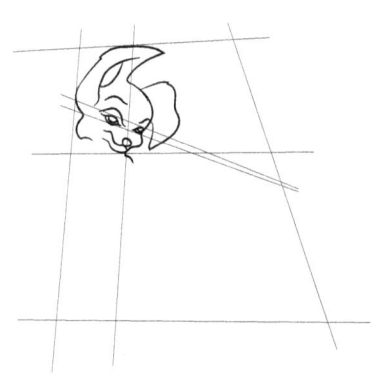
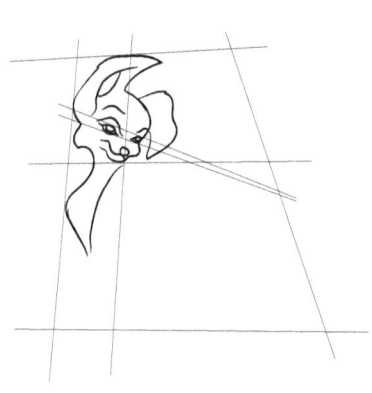
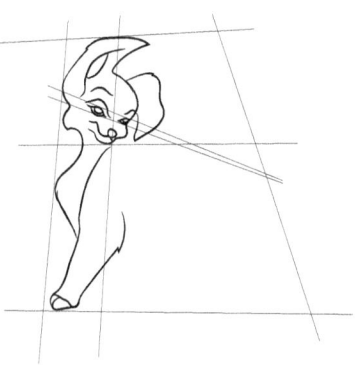

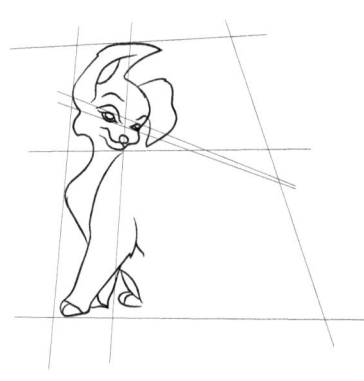

How to draw a dog using a grid. You can download blank grids to practice with in dark and light PDF formats by following the link below.

https://www.lipdf.com/product/grids/

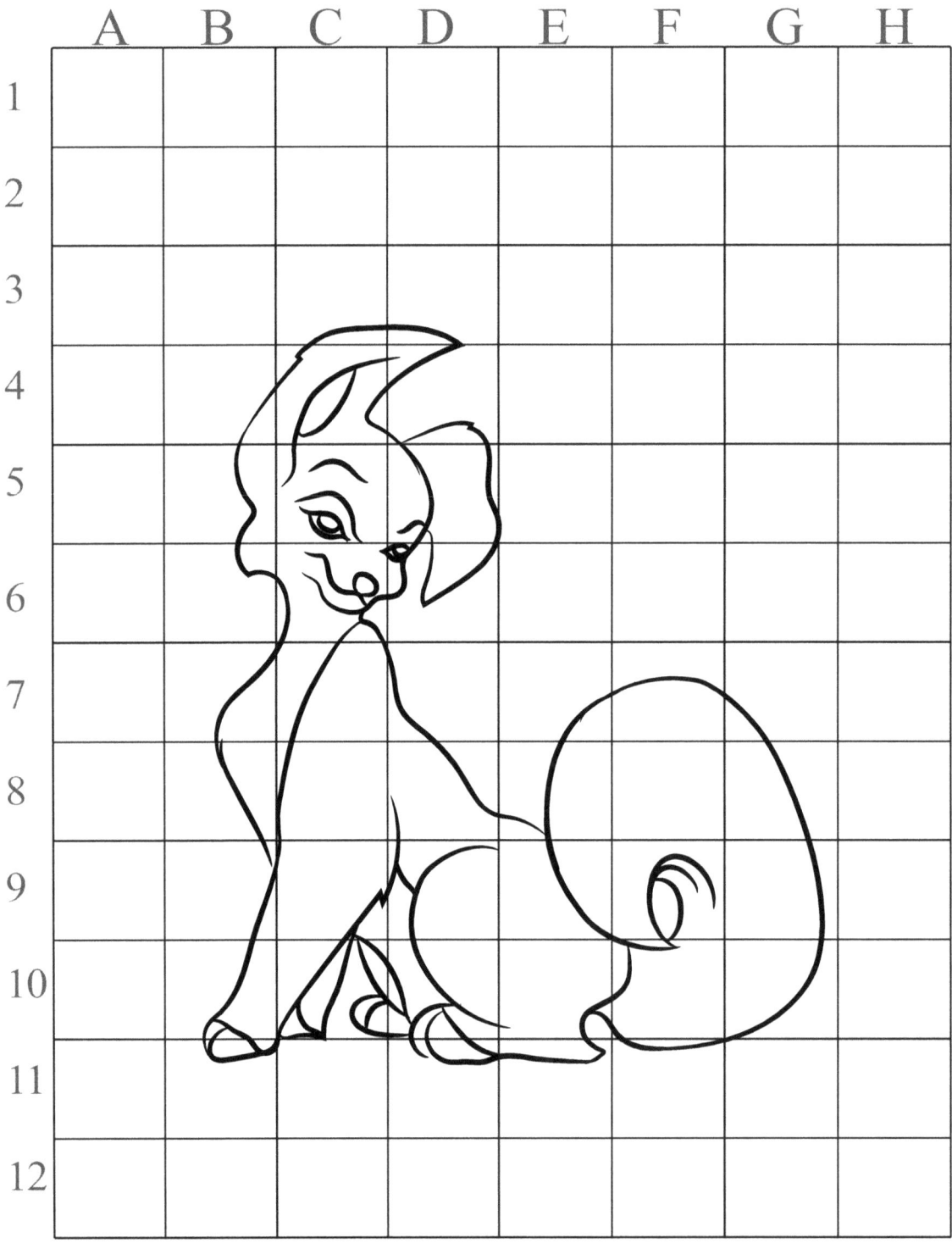

28. The use of ellipses in grids can be very helpful when you want to create round shapes.

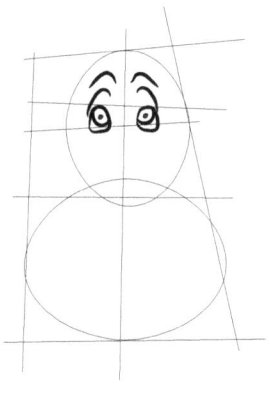 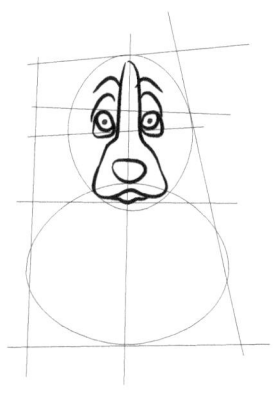 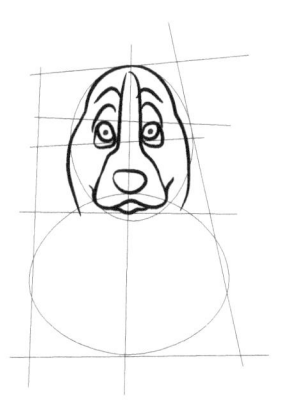

How to draw a dog using a grid. You can download blank grids to practice with in dark and light PDF formats by following the link below.

https://www.lipdf.com/product/grids/

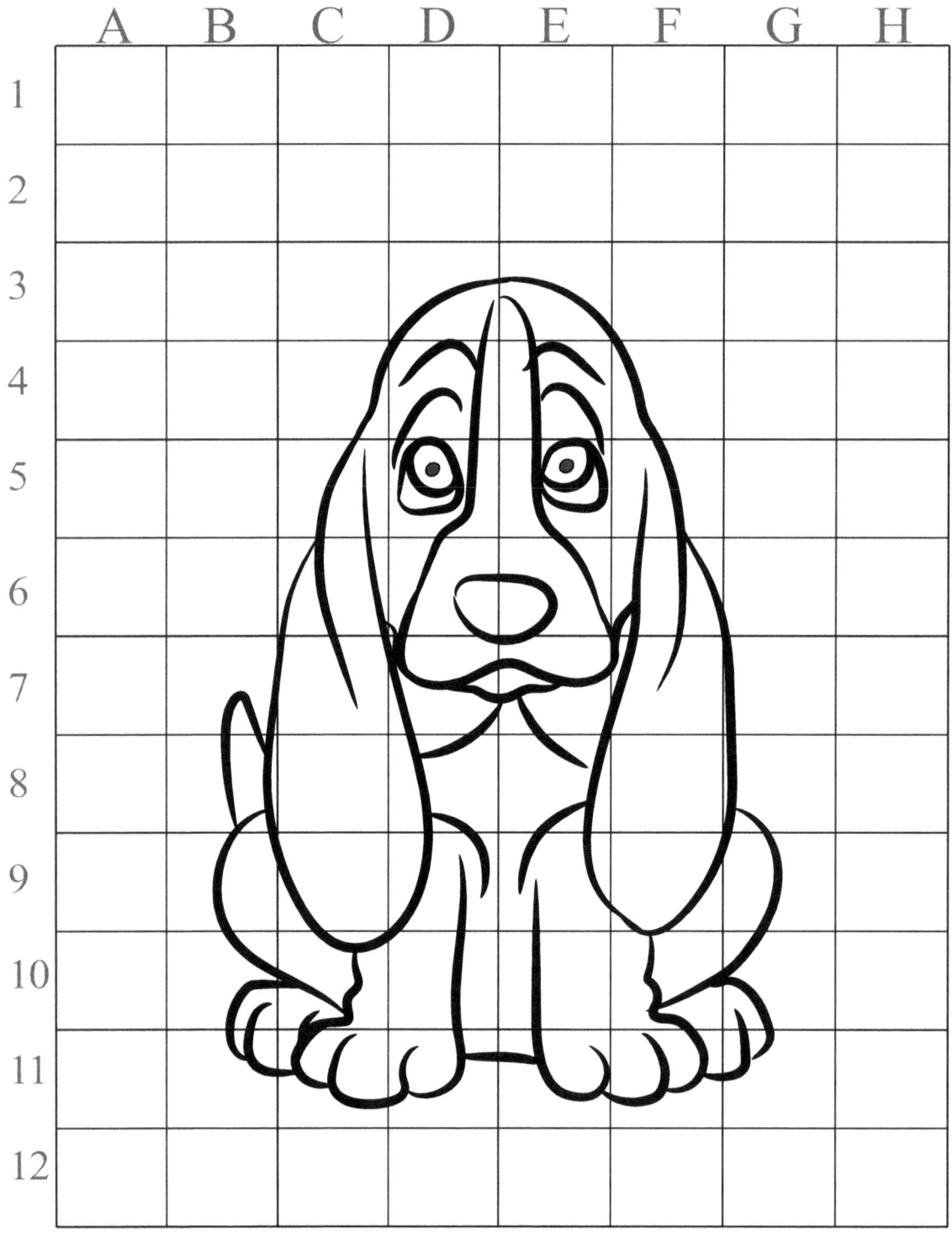

29. You can change the features of your character by lengthening some parts and shortening others.

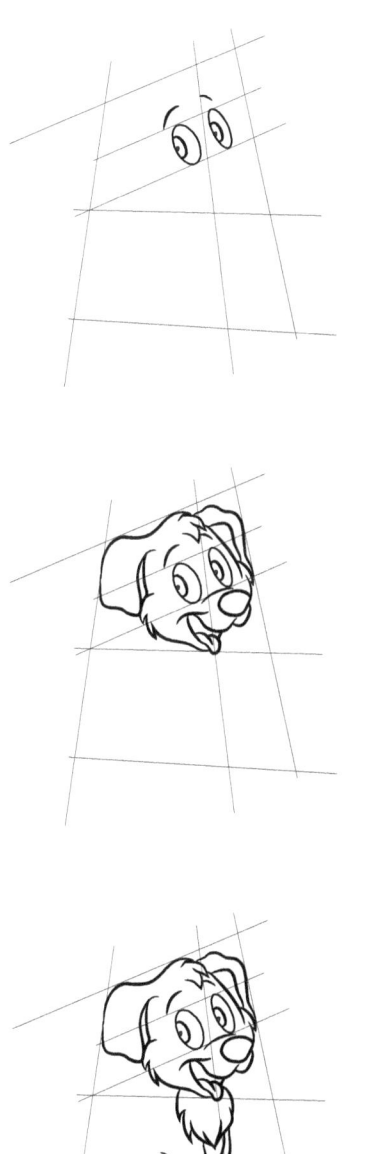

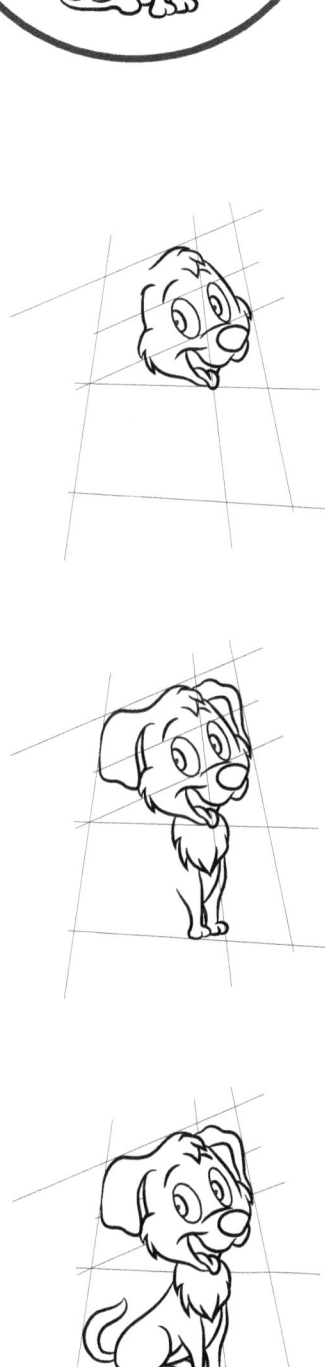

How to draw a dog using a grid. You can download blank grids to practice with in dark and light PDF formats by following the link below.

https://www.lipdf.com/product/grids/

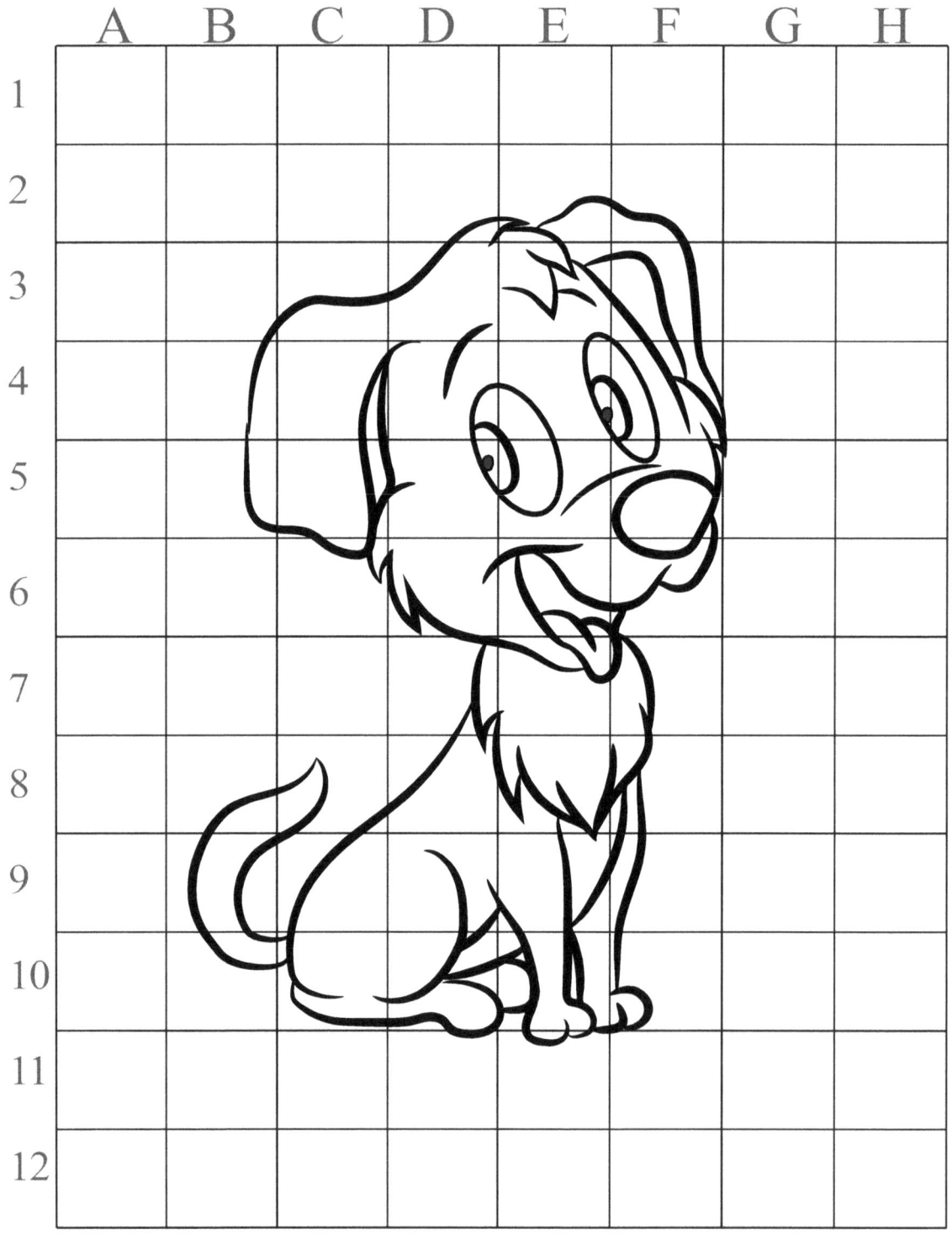

30. Try altering your grid to make your character shorter or taller.

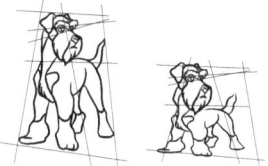

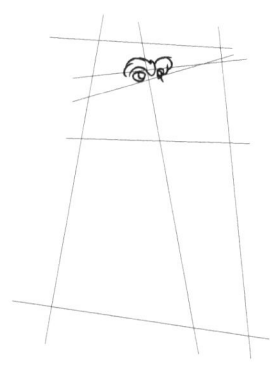
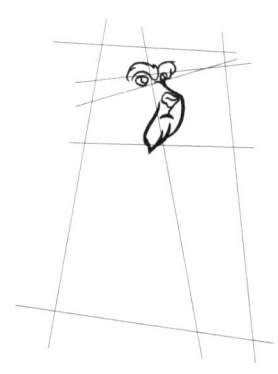
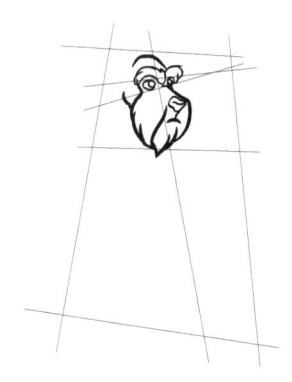

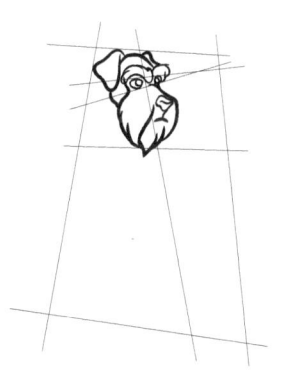
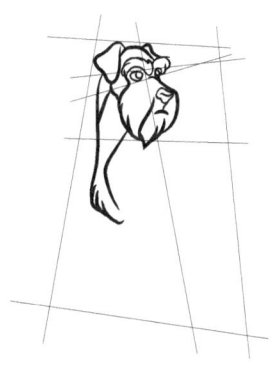

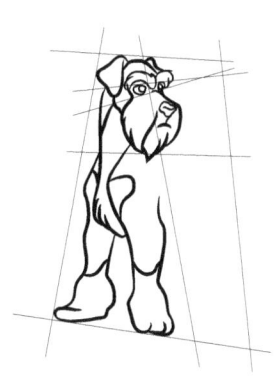

How to draw a dog using a grid. You can download blank grids to practice with in dark and light PDF formats by following the link below.

https://www.lipdf.com/product/grids/

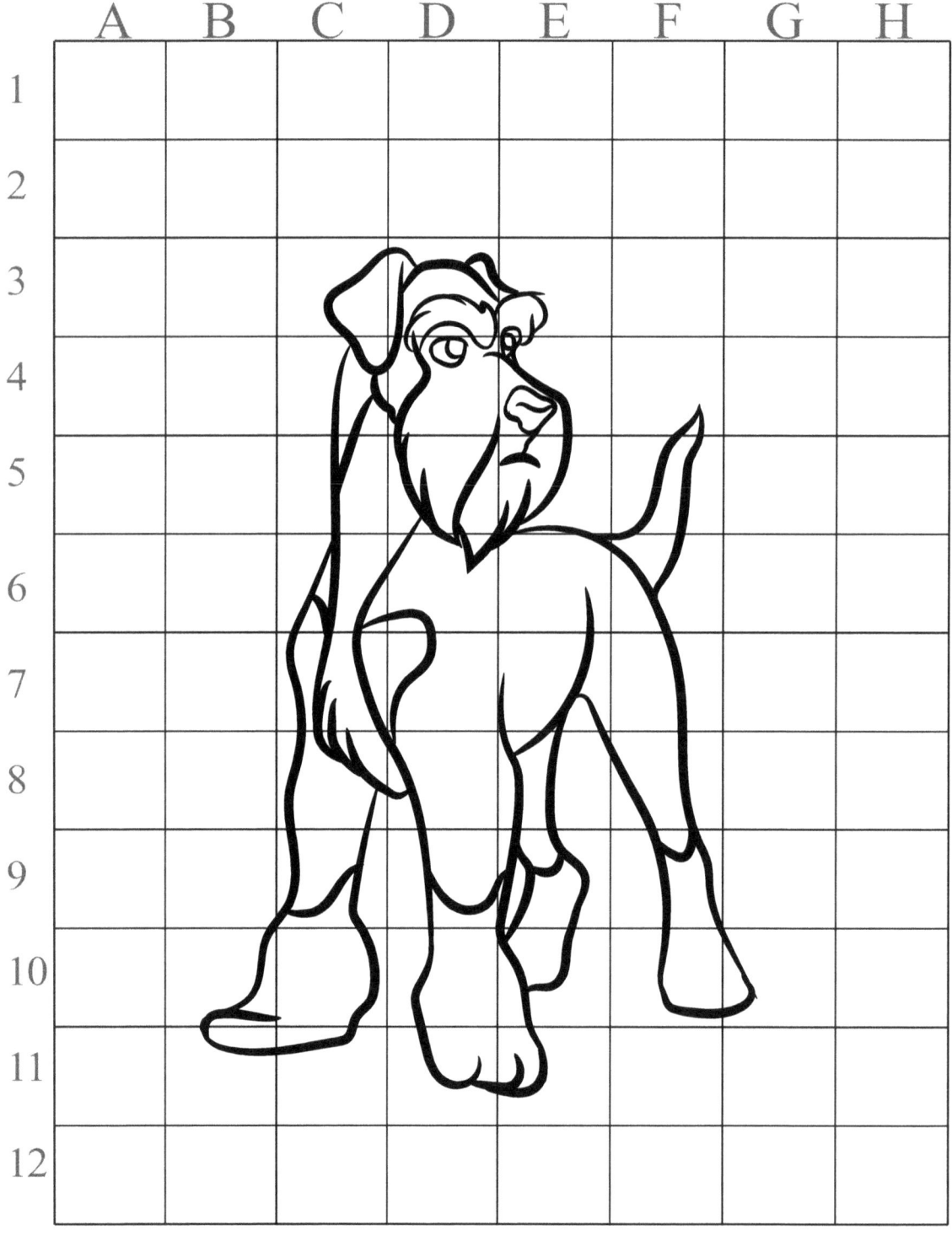

31. Extend or reduce the width of your grid to make changes to your character.

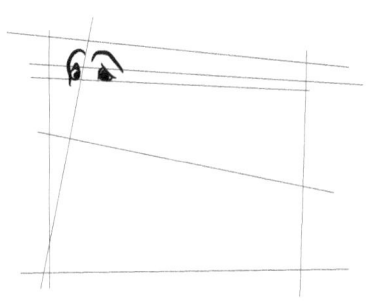

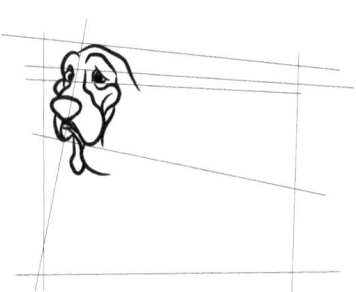

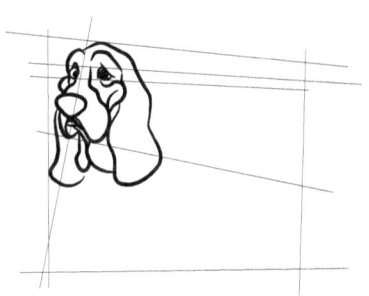

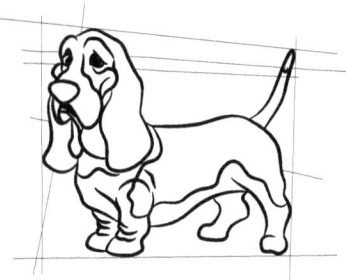

How to draw a dog using a grid. You can download blank grids to practice with in dark and light PDF formats by following the link below.

https://www.lipdf.com/product/grids/

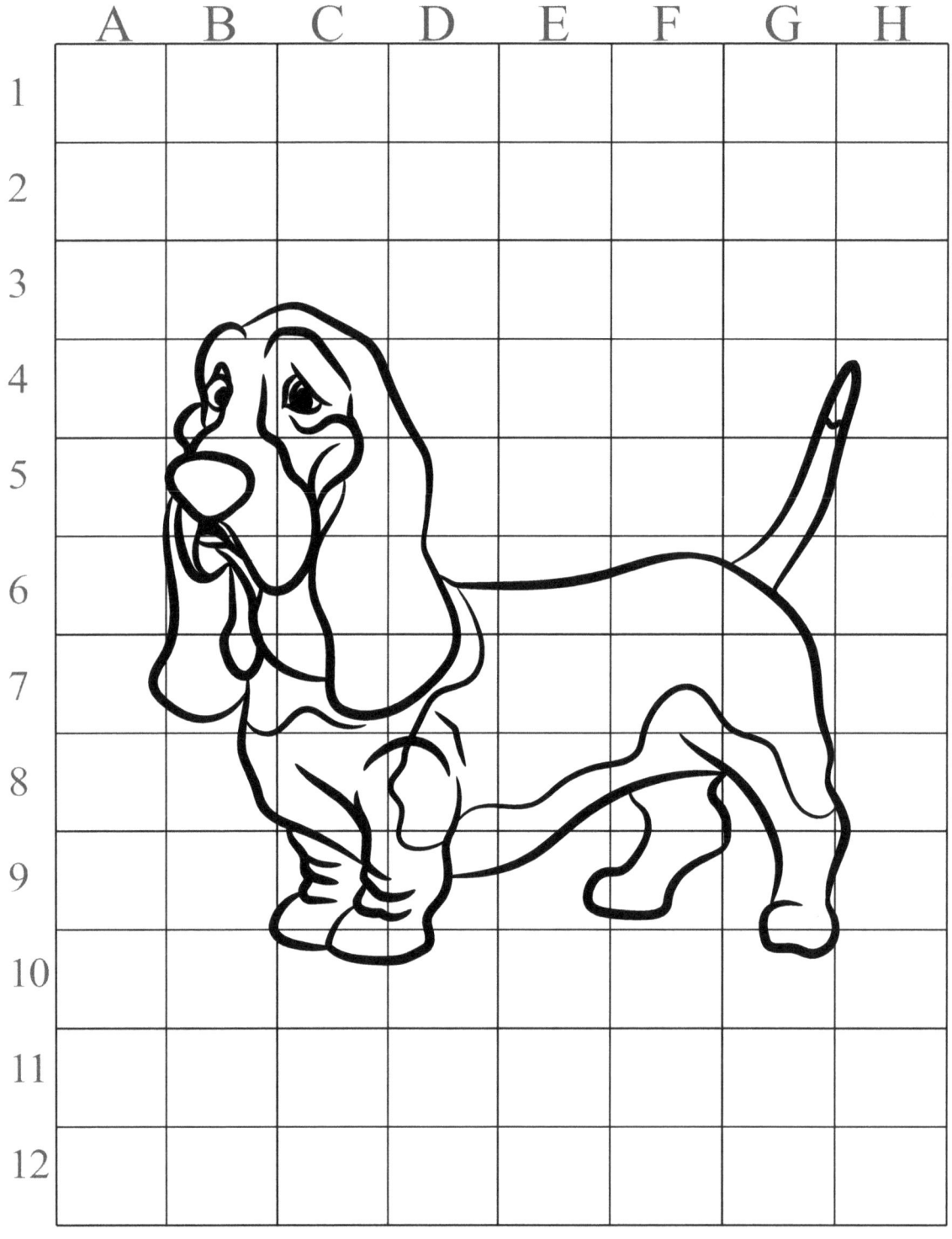

32. A simple grid can often help to guide you when drawing. After you have drawn your grid, begin with the eyes.

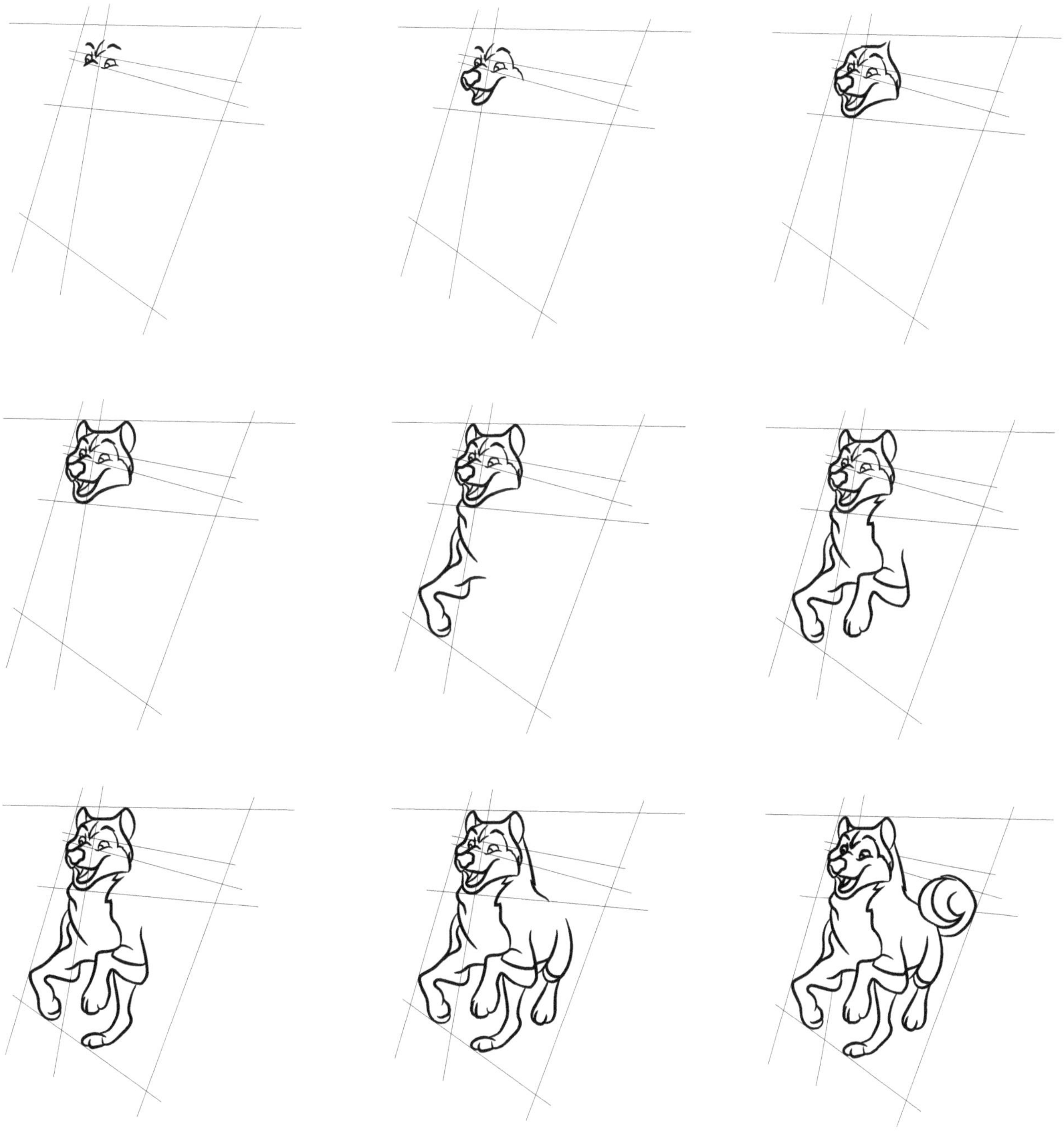

How to draw a dog using a grid. You can download blank grids to practice with in dark and light PDF formats by following the link below.

https://www.lipdf.com/product/grids/

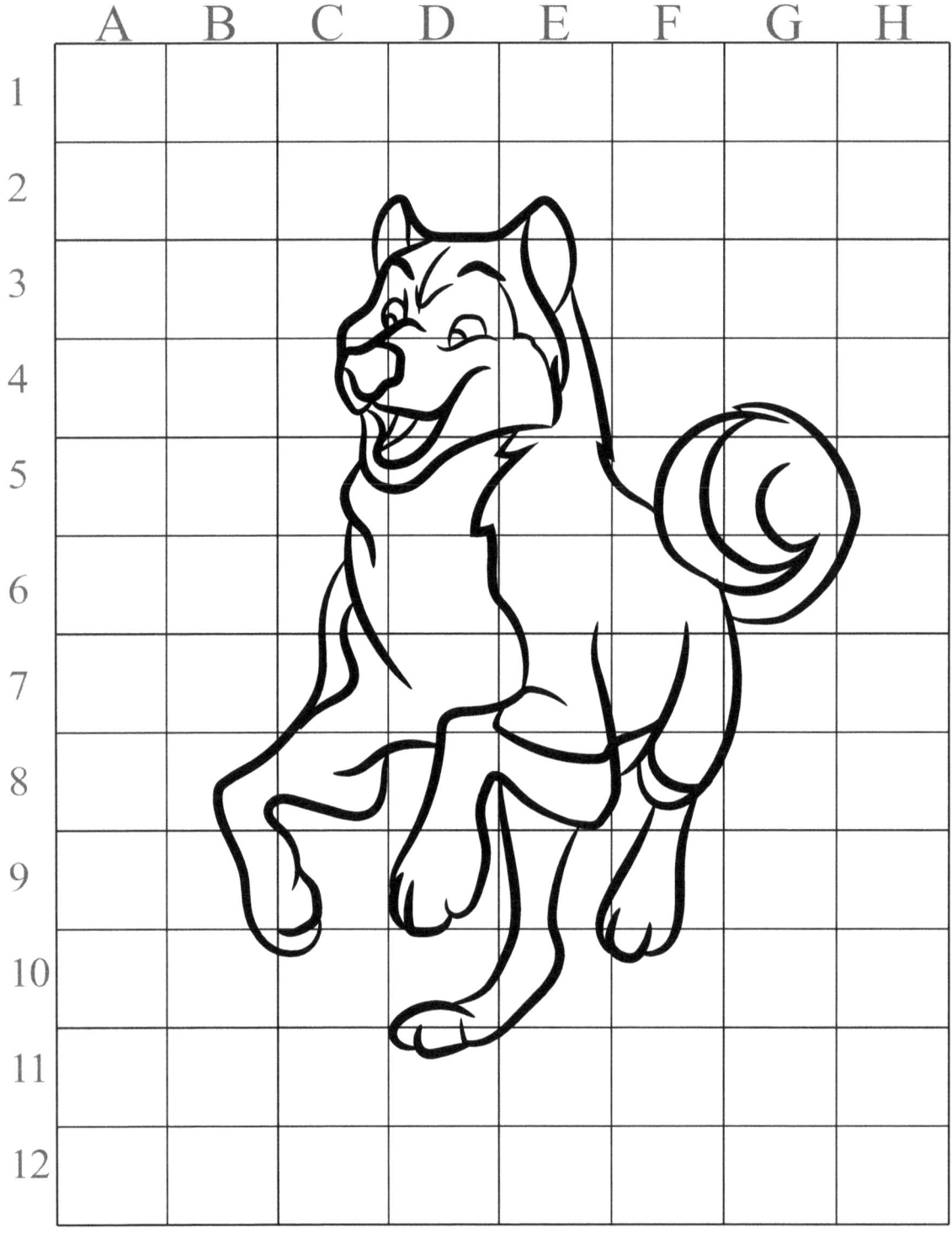

33. Drawing a basic grid outline will help you to give your picture good proportions.

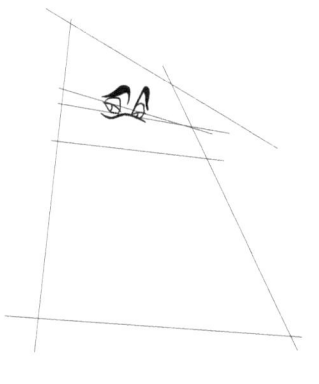 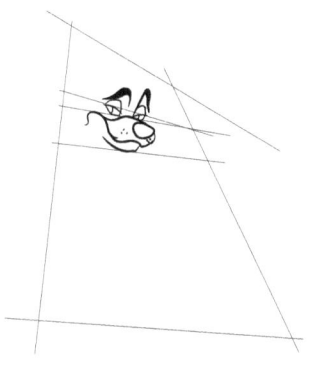 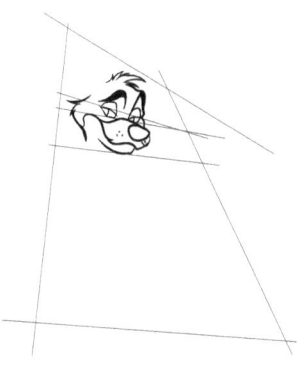

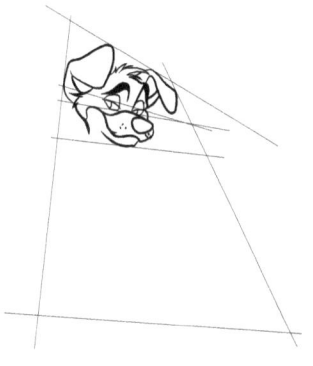 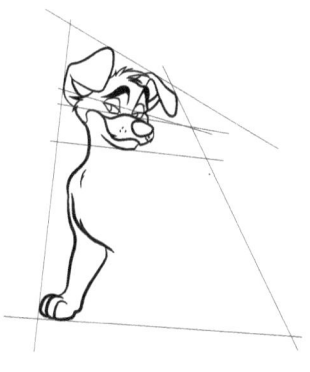 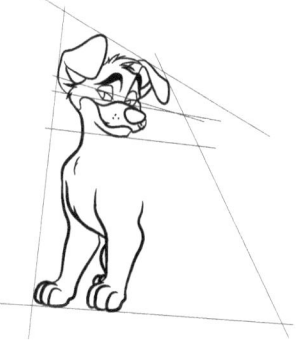

How to draw a dog using a grid. You can download blank grids to practice with in dark and light PDF formats by following the link below.

https://www.lipdf.com/product/grids/

34. Try changing your character's features to create alternative versions.

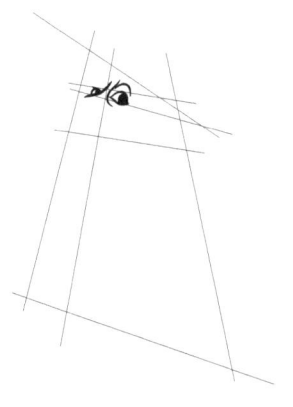
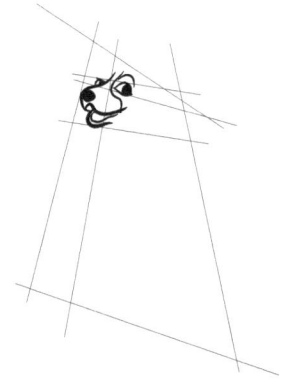
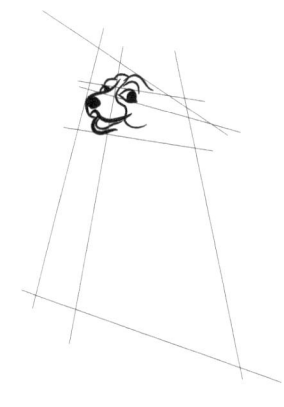
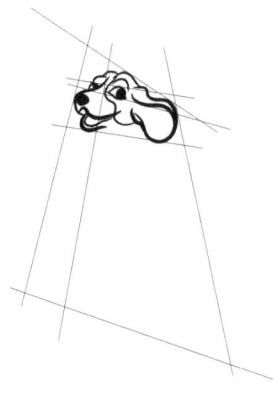

How to draw a dog using a grid. You can download blank grids to practice with in dark and light PDF formats by following the link below.

https://www.lipdf.com/product/grids/

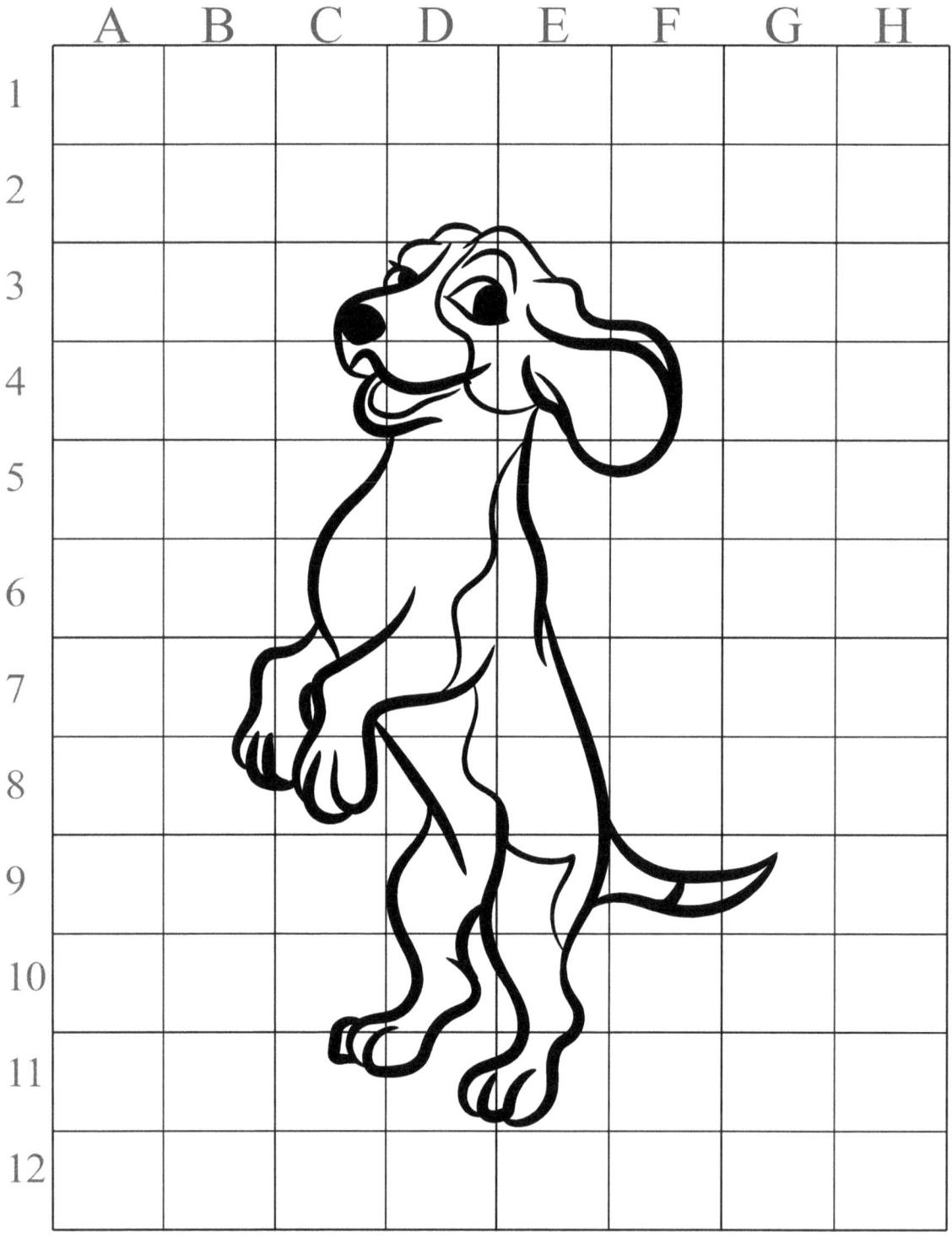

35. Ellipses in your grid can make it easier to keep your character in proportion.

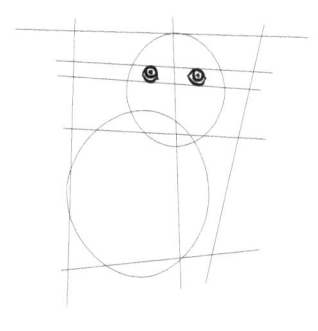
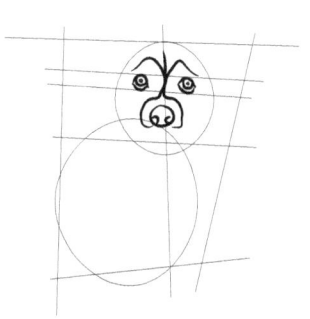
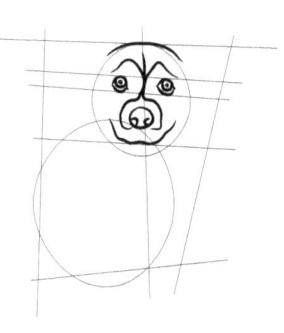

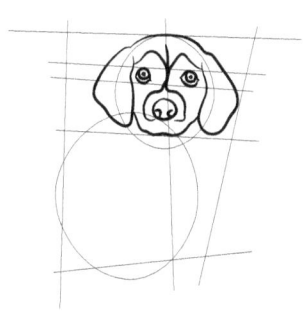

How to draw a dog using a grid. You can download blank grids to practice with in dark and light PDF formats by following the link below.

https://www.lipdf.com/product/grids/

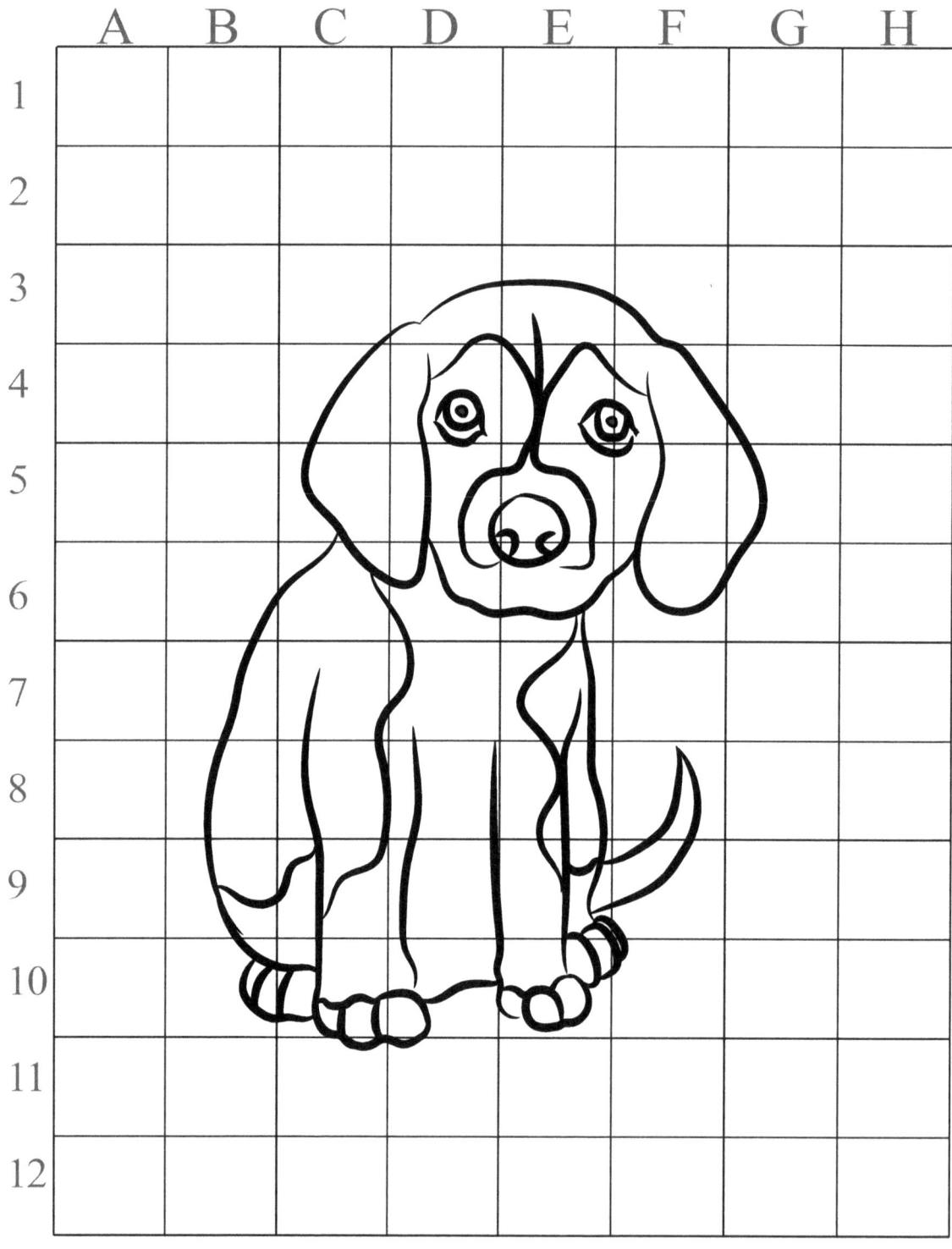

36. You can make your character's head stand out more by creating a larger area of overlap on your ellipses.

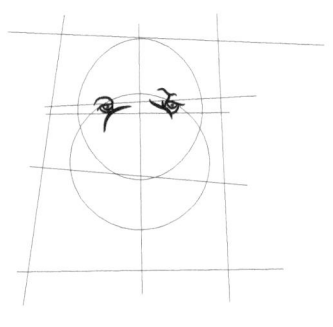
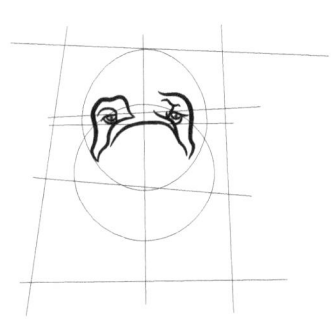
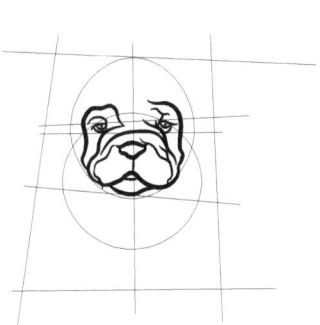

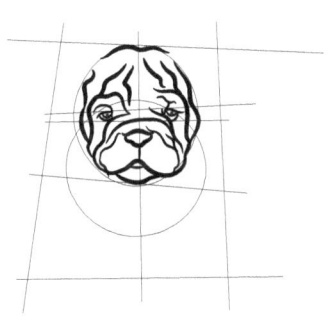
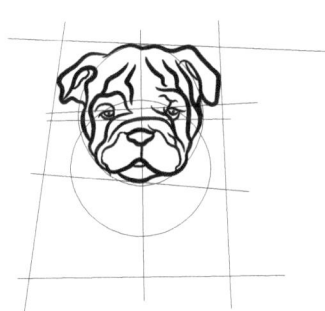

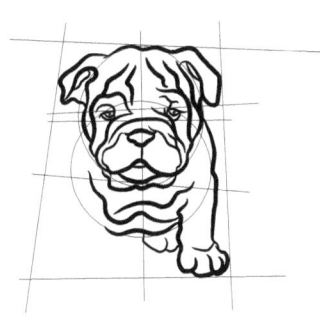

How to draw a dog using a grid. You can download blank grids to practice with in dark and light PDF formats by following the link below.

https://www.lipdf.com/product/grids/

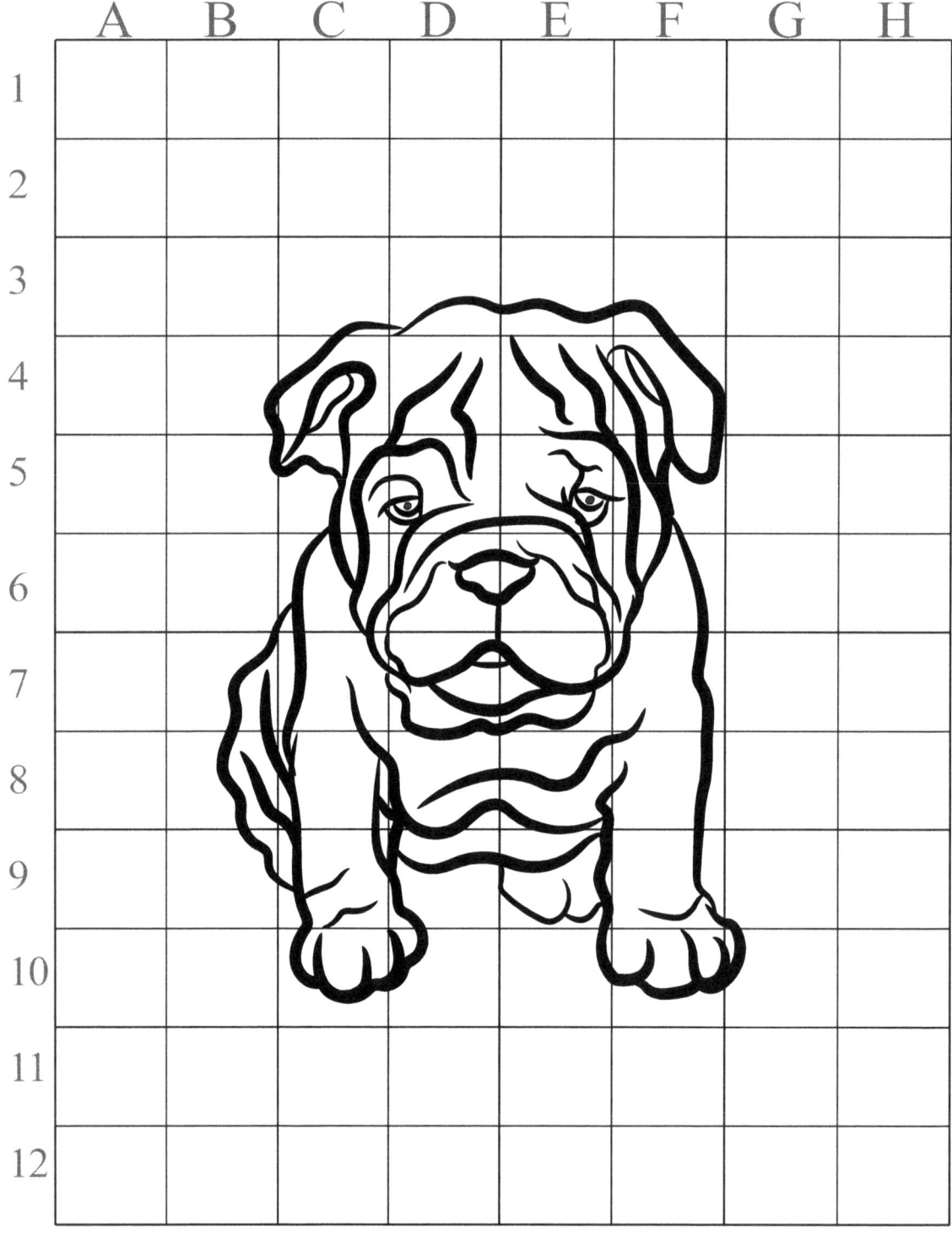

37. Ellipses on your initial grid can be used to help you draw characters with a 3D effect.

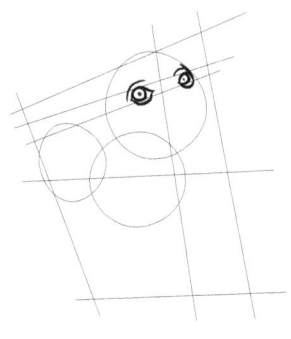 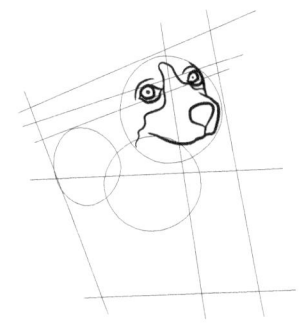 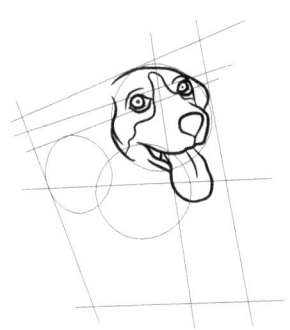

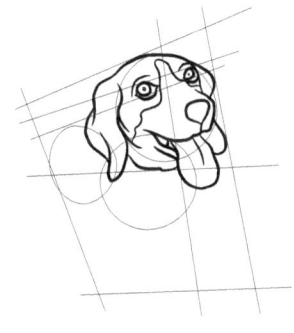 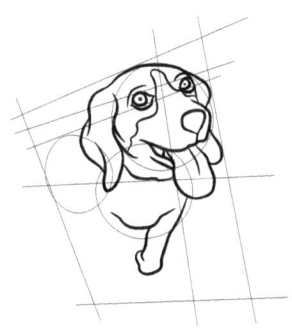 

How to draw a dog using a grid. You can download blank grids to practice with in dark and light PDF formats by following the link below.

https://www.lipdf.com/product/grids/

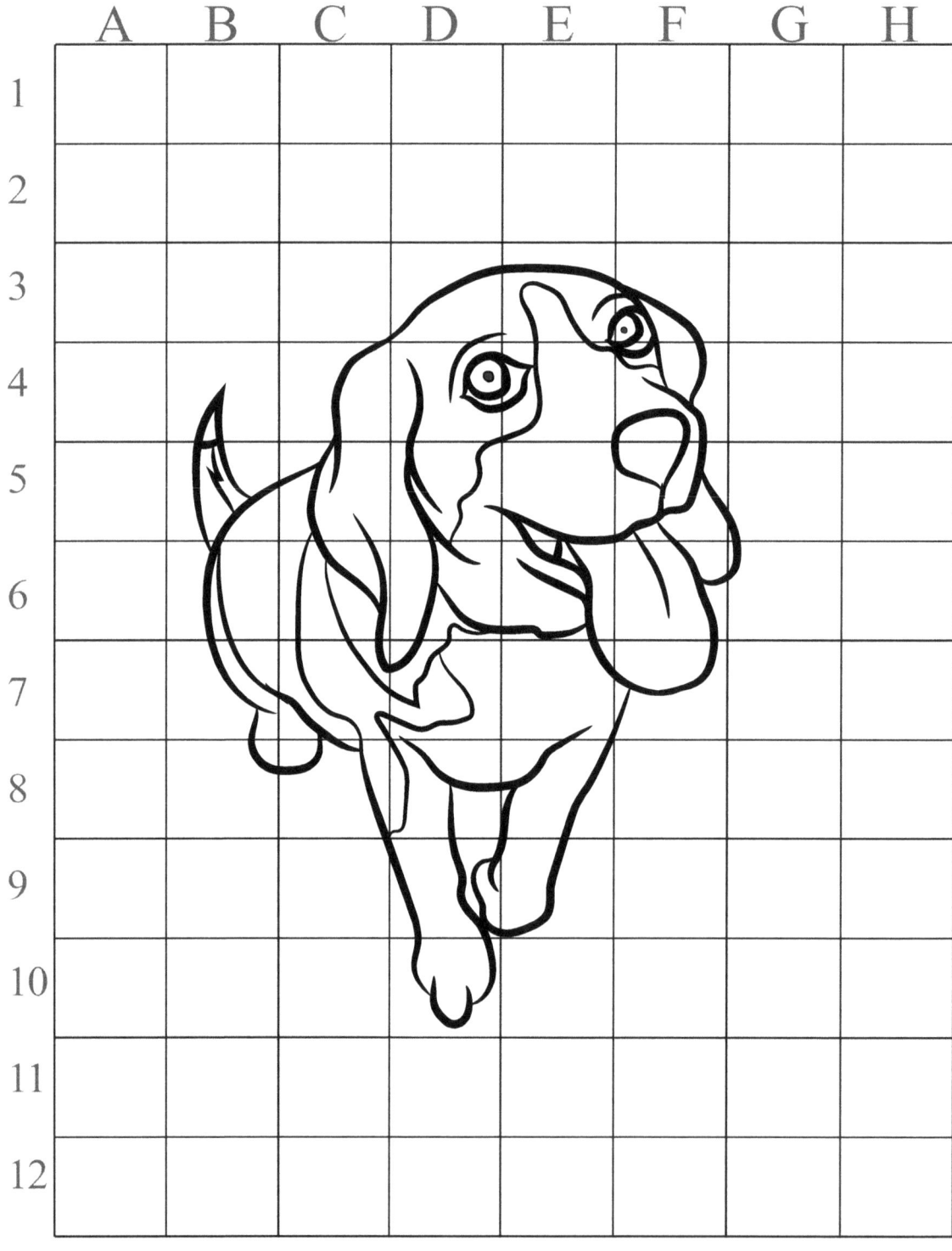

38. Bonus Picture. How to draw a simple dinosaur. On your grid you can add an arc to help guide you with the curve of your dinosaur's tail.

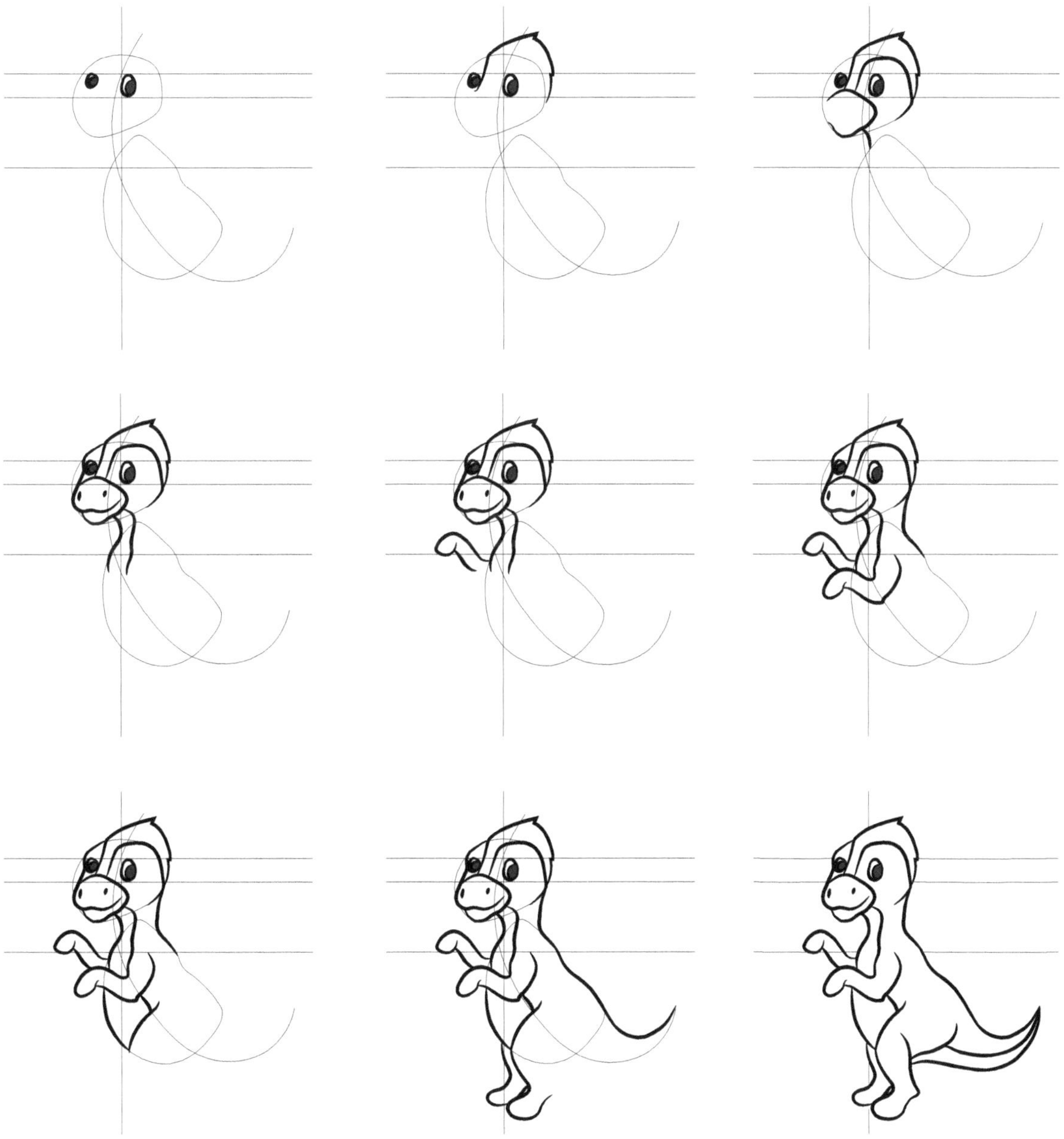

How to draw a dinosaur using a grid. You can download blank grids to practice with in dark and light PDF formats by following the link below.

https://www.lipdf.com/product/grids/

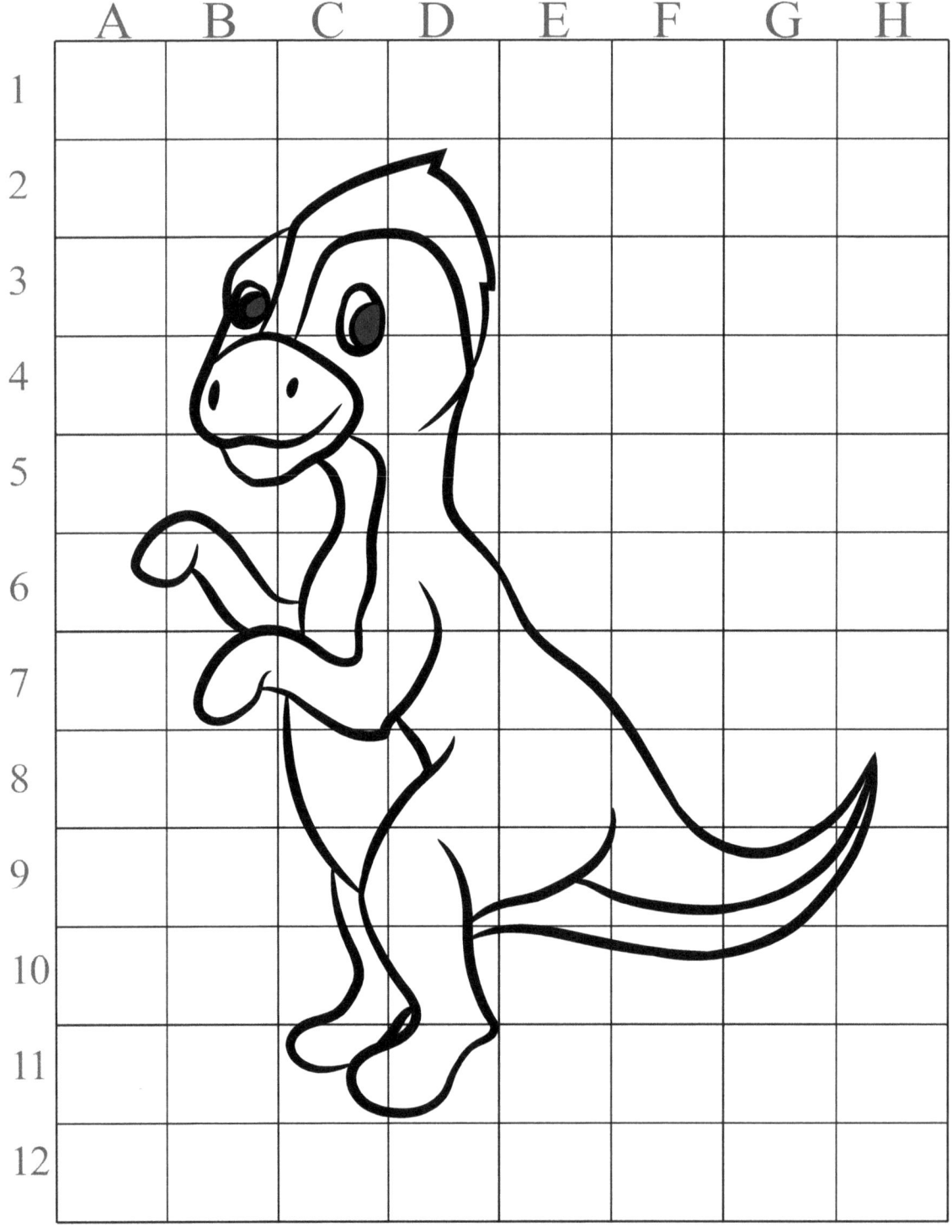

CPSIA information can be obtained
at www.ICGtesting.com
Printed in the USA
LVHW060417241121
704333LV00021B/340